THE NINE-FOLD ASCENT

LEVELS OF MIGRATION ON THE SUFI PATH TO GOD

SHAYKH MUHAMMAD HISHAM KABBANI

INSTITUTE FOR SPIRITUAL AND CULTURAL ADVANCEMENT

Library of Congress Cataloging-in-Publication Data

Published and Distributed by:
Institute for Spiritual and Cultural Advancement

17195 Silver Parkway, #401
Fenton, MI 48430 USA
Tel: (888) 278-6624
Fax:(810) 815-0518
Email: staff@Naqshbandi.org
Web: http://www.Naqshbandi.org

First Edition: July 2009
ISBN: 978-1-930409-59-0

Contents

Publisher's Notes 7
Universally Recognized Symbols 8
Transliteration 8

About the Author x

Foreword 12

Introduction to the Nine Steps: from Initiation to Divine Support 19
Angels of Answering 25
A Rope, an Axe, and a Night in a Grave 33
Bahlul's House in Paradise 35

The First Level 43
The First Step: Initiation 43
The Second Step: Submission 45
Keep Full Presence 48
Step Three: The Right Path 50
Step Four: *Taqwa* 51
Step Five: Divine Support 52

The Second Level—Your Daily Personal Liturgy 54
Prescription to Atomize 54
Safeguard Your Heart with the Daily Personal Liturgy 58
More on the Daily Liturgy Prescribed by Your Shaykh 59
Penalty for Leaving the Daily Personal Liturgy 73
How to Make Up for a Day of Missed Daily Personal Liturgy 74

The Third Level—Sincerity, Witnessing, God's Holy Name, Purification 76

The Fourth Level—the Station of Gnosis 83

The Fifth Level—Breaking Anger and Obliterating the Ego 91
Falsehood and Truth 95
Thankful Rich 98
The Story of the Wrestler and the Apple Tree 99

The Sixth Level—Energy, Ablution, and Communication by Light . 104

The Seventh Level—Strict Awareness of *Halal* and *Haram* 113

Shaykh Muhammad Nazim Adil al-Ḥaqqani (right), world leader of the most distinguished Naqshbandi-Ḥaqqani Sufi Order, with his representative, and author of this book, Shaykh Muhammad Hisham Kabbani.

بسم الله الرحمن الرحيم

لَتَرْكَبُنَّ طَبَقًا عَن طَبَقٍ

Ye shall surely travel from stage to stage.

Holy Qur'an: Sūratu 'l-Inshiqāq (Cleft Asunder), 84:19

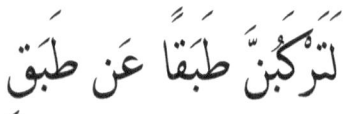

PUBLISHER'S NOTES

This book is specifically designed for laypersons and readers unfamiliar with Sufi terms. As such, we have occasionally replaced Arabic terminology with English translations, except in instances where Arabic terms are crucial to the tone and substance of the text. In such instances, we have included transliterations or footnoted explanations.

As the source material is an oral transmission, its language was revised for a written format, and references have been added as appropriate; however, we have tried our best to retain the essence of the author's original talks. We ask the reader's forgiveness for any omissions in this final text.

Qur'anic quotes are centered, highlighted in italics and footnoted, citing chapter name, number and verse. The Holy Traditions of Prophet Muhammad ﷺ (known as *hadith*) are footnoted, where possible, referencing the books in which they are cited.

Where gender-specific pronouns such as "he" and "him" are applied in a general sense, it has been solely for the flow of text, and no discrimination is intended towards female readers.

Universally Recognized Symbols

The following Arabic symbols connote sacredness and are universally recognized by Sufi Muslims:

The symbol ﷾ represents *subhanahu wa taʿala*, a high form of praise reserved for God alone, which is customarily recited after reading or pronouncing the common name Allah, and any of the ninety-nine Islamic Holy Names of God.

The symbol ﷺ represents *sall-allahu ʿalayhi wa sallam* (God's blessings and greetings of peace be upon the Prophet), which is customarily recited after reading or pronouncing the holy name of Prophet Muhammad.

The symbol ؑ represents *ʿalayhi 's-salam* (peace be upon him/her), which is customarily recited after reading or pronouncing the sanctified names of prophets, Prophet Muhammad's family members, and the angels.

The symbol ؓ represents *radi-allahu ʿanh/ʿanha* (may God be pleased with him/her), which is customarily recited after reading or pronouncing the holy names of Prophet Muhammad's Companions.

The symbol ق represents *qaddas-allahu sirrah* (may God sanctify his or her secret), which is customarily recited after reading or pronouncing the name of a saint.

Transliteration

Arabic names, places and terms are transliterated in the main text and the Glossary to facilitate correct pronunciation based on the following system:

Symbol	Transliteration	Symbol	Transliteration	Vowels: Long	
ء	'	ط	ṭ	آ ى	ā
ب	b	ظ	ẓ	و	ū
ت	t	ع	ʿ	ي	ī
ث	th	غ	gh	**Short**	
ج	j	ف	f	َ	a
ح	ḥ	ق	q	ُ	u
خ	kh	ك	k	ِ	i
د	d	ل	l		
ذ	dh	م	m		
ر	r	ن	n		
ز	z	ه	h		
س	s	و	w		
ش	sh	ي	y		
ص	ṣ	ة	ah; at		
ض	ḍ	ال	al-/'l-		

About the Author

Shaykh Muhammad Hisham Kabbani is a world-renowned author and religious scholar. He has devoted his life to the promotion of the traditional Islamic principles of peace, tolerance, love, compassion and brotherhood, while opposing extremism in all its forms. The shaykh is a member of a respected family of traditional Islamic scholars, which includes the former head of the Association of Muslim Scholars of Lebanon and the present Grand Mufti[1] of Lebanon.

In the U.S., Shaykh Kabbani serves as Chairman, Islamic Supreme Council of America; Founder, Naqshbandi Sufi Order of America; Advisor, World Organization for Resource Development and Education; Chairman, As-Sunnah Foundation of America; Chairman, Kamilat Muslim Women's Organization; and, Founder and President, The Muslim Magazine.

Shaykh Kabbani is highly trained, both as a Western scientist and as a classical Islamic scholar. He received a bachelor's degree in chemistry and studied medicine. In addition, he also holds a degree in Islamic Divine Law, and under the tutelage of Shaykh ʿAbd Allah Daghestani ق, license to teach, guide and counsel religious students in Islamic spirituality from Shaykh Muhammad Nazim ʿAdil al-Qubrusi al-Ḥaqqani an-Naqshbandi ق, the world leader of the Naqshbandi-Ḥaqqani Sufi Order.

His books include: *A Spiritual Commentary on the Chapter of Sincerity (2006)*, *Sufi Science of Self-Realization* (Fons Vitae, 2005), *Keys to the Divine Kingdom* (2005); *Classical Islam and the Naqshbandi*

---

[1] The highest Islamic religious authority in the country.

Sufi Order (2004); *The Naqshbandi Sufi Tradition Guidebook* (2004); *The Approach of Armageddon? An Islamic Perspective* (2003); *Encyclopedia of Muhammad's Women Companions and the Traditions They Related* (1998, with Dr. Laleh Bakhtiar); *Encyclopedia of Islamic Doctrine* (7 vols. 1998); *Angels Unveiled* (1996); *The Naqshbandi Sufi Way* (1995); *Remembrance of God Liturgy of the Sufi Naqshbandi Masters* (1994).

In his long-standing endeavor to promote better understanding of classical Islam, Shaykh Kabbani has hosted two international conferences in the United States, both of which drew scholars from throughout the Muslim world. As a resounding voice for traditional Islam, his counsel is sought by journalists, academics and government leaders.

Foreword

Sainthood is not a joke, nor is the power of Guidance. It is not for just anyone to claim the power to guide. It is very important to connect to a genuine shaykh. If you connect with a real shaykh, you can fly. But if you connect with a shaykh who, though pious, has not reached true sainthood, you will only be walking. That is because the saintly shaykhs are connected to the Divine Presence.

Someone who is a true saint possesses six powers. These powers enable the saint, when he opens his mouth to speak, is able to reach whoever has "receivers" and who listen to that "broadcast" from the main station. At that time, the saint is the source, no longer transmitting what was said by others.

Today, they have live broadcasts and recorded broadcasts. The recorded ones are excerpted from live broadcasts. The resulting recording may be outdated and old-fashioned, like old tape recorders; half-way through, the tape may break, and then you have to splice it back together. The Shaykh of Blessing (*Shaykh al-Baraka*) is like that. However, with the shaykh that is connected to the Divine Presence, angels, spiritual beings and saints are all listening to him, receiving information when he speaks.

As soon as you say *"Allah,"* anyone with a receiver can receive. It is a wave. It does not die, it continues. That is why it is always being written. If you program your computer to say *"Allah □ Allah □,"* it will keep doing so until Judgment Day without stopping. That wavelength mentioning the Name *"Allah"* is moving. You can receive that wavelength if you have a receiver and extract the sound from it. That is the big difference between a true Shaykh of Guidance (*irshād*) and a Shaykh of Blessing.

For one on the real path to sainthood, the first level to be achieved is wakefulness. This is the level of readiness and awareness—awareness of God's Divine Presence, of His watching you. One who has reached that level is always aware of what is going to happen. You must be aware of everything around you that takes you away from God.

Beware, because at any moment your ego may bring you down. Do not let the "donkeyness" of your ego overcome you. Do not allow your ego to order you to do this or that. You have to submit to God. If you listen to and obey your ego's whims and desires, running towards what it wants and fleeing what it hates, then watch out. A moment of heedlessness might be enough to destroy you completely. That is why you need a guide.

Take the analogy of a lawyer. To protect his clients, a lawyer may tell him not to do things that, though they may seem innocuous, are in fact illegal. He, or she, may advise against things that are technically legal, but have the appearance of impropriety or illegality. He may advise against legal actions that could lead to unlawful behavior. The lawyer wants to eliminate any chance that his client will be sued or face criminal prosecution. Thus, a lawyer becomes an instrument for informing his client about these pitfalls and preventing them from transgressing into unlawful behavior. Lawyers remind you. They know that one mistake is enough. You might make a thousand mistakes without being seen, but if one of those mistakes is discovered, then you will be in trouble.

Similarly, if you drive your car with a police officer sitting beside you in the passenger seat, you will not drive too fast, but dutifully observe all the rules and regulations of the road. Knowing that he would stop you, you refrain.

The tricks of Satan and the ego can make you fall immediately. Not having a spiritual "lawyer," a guide, is like being heedless of the laws that the police around you enforce. A real shaykh is such a spiritual advocate. Using the powers of telepathy (see Reality of Focusing) that God bestowed upon him, he is able to warn you. He is able to communicate through your heart, even when he is far away, helping you remain aware and avoid heedlessness. Thus, you become conscious of anything that might lead you into error. In this way, enlightenment begins to take over your heart.

Perhaps *all* our actions are heedless, and perhaps they might all pass by, unseen or forgiven. But one heedless act that is not forgiven can destroy us completely. The guide keeps us from that one act, just as the lawyer protects us from behavior that transgresses the law. We are under the shaykh's microscope, and he is checking us.

This is the first of the ten different levels on the way of gnostics that you must achieve. Reach these ten levels, and only then will you open the six powers that are in your heart.

We must focus our attention on the same point that all Muslims focus on, the Holy Mosque in Mecca, *Masjid al-Ḥarām*. That is the place where no sin can be committed. The heart of the believer must be treated the same way, for God said, "My heavens and My Earth cannot contain Me, but the heart of My believer can contain Me." By following this Way, the heart becomes like the *Masjid al-Ḥarām*, a place where sins are prohibited. It becomes a place dedicated to God.

> The Prophet Muhammad ﷺ said:
> There is not one among you but a comrade from among the jinn is assigned to him." They (the Companions present) said: "Even you, O Messenger of God?" He ﷺ said: "Even me, but God granted me victory over him and he became Muslim, so he only enjoins me to do that which is good.[2]

---

[2] Muslim.

We cannot throw our devils out, but we have to keep struggling against them. We are weak servants. O our Lord, if You do not support us, we fail; with Your support, we succeed.

In Islam, we know that there are 500 good actions to be done and 800 forbidden actions that the Prophet ﷺ ordered us to avoid. Before you begin to meditate on God through *dhikr*, you have to meditate on how to throw the dirt—your donkey-like characteristics and ignorance—from your heart. That is why the Prophet ﷺ said, "To contemplate for one hour is better than seventy years of worship."

Audit yourself. If the government tax office comes and says, "We want to audit you," what would you do? You would be worried that they might find a mistake, even though you tried your best not to make any mistakes. You might tremble. If you tremble before the tax auditor, how do you think you will be before God, when He calls you to be audited?

Then shall anyone who has done an atom's weight of good, see it![3]

Do you not believe in the Day that is coming? For saints, that Day is every day. Their disciples must audit themselves. If you audit yourself, it is as if you prayed for seventy years.

One time Grandshaykh 'Abd Allah ق said, "It is very easy to pray two cycles of prayer or to fast one day, but it is very difficult to leave one forbidden action." For example, you look at something forbidden and keep looking, because your ego does not let you stop. All of us are dipped and dumped in forbidden actions. Anger is one of the worst characteristics. The Prophet Muhammad ﷺ said, *"Anger is unbelief."* Who does not have anger? You cannot claim that you do not have it; the truth is that you blow up at everyone.

---

[3] Sūratu 'l-Zalzalah (The Earthquake), 99:7.

It is most important to look at our negative characteristics. The shaykh, when he looks at you, knows what kind of negativity you are harboring. The Naqshbandi masters have determined that four major factors influence every human being's character. These are lust, the ego, worldly desire and the whispers of Satan. This book addresses the latter three factors: ego, worldly desire and Satan's influence.

When someone begins to consider taking up the Path to the Divine Presence and following the way of Gnosticism, the ruinous characteristics of the self become obstacles which must be eliminated. This process of wayfaring is known as seeking the Station of Perfected Character, *Ihsan*.

Initially, when the spirituality of the individual begins to call him and his soul begins yearning for its heavenly spiritual connection, it will begin to impact not only his psyche and emotional state, but also his body. At that time, the individual begins to realize there is a need to develop the spiritual dimension and he begins to search for a spiritual master to guide him. Ultimately, that yearning will overwhelm him and he will begin to search in earnest for such guidance.

As soon as he begins that search, heavenly power from the Divine Presence will direct him to his spiritual guide, who is a master of the Path. Love will then begin to develop between the seeker and that guide, and in his heart he will grow connected to his master. As that relationship of love begins to grow, he begins to look at the personality of his teacher with great love. This love develops into a spiritual connection, so that he begins his spiritual journey in the state of unconditional love. Such love is not related to any desire, but is a purely Platonic, spiritual love between the teacher and the student. Thus, he enters what is known as the, the Circle of Unconditional Lovers, (*dā'irat al-muḥibīn*). That is the circle of students at the first level of the Way: the Level of Love.

When that love begins to appear in him, the master is the center of the circle, and the students are each a point on its circumference. Each has his or her own connection to the center, the master. That means each has his own direction, or *qiblah,* that points towards his teacher. As that connection begins to become apparent to the seeker—as for the master, it has always been so—that radius becomes like a bridge or tunnel into which the seeker begins to step from the circumference of the circle. Upon making his first steps into that tunnel, he begins to discover countless bad characteristics within himself. These negative traits can be condensed into seventeen primary characteristics. He might possess some or all of the seventeen within himself. The student then begins to realize that his teacher does not possess these characteristics. As he discovers one characteristic after another, he begins to eliminate them. As he begins to eliminate them, he moves down the tunnel and becomes a "beginner in the circle of lovers on the spiritual journey."

Once he becomes a beginner, he needs to achieve nine steps to reach the level of disciple. Eliminating the seventeen characteristics takes the seeker from the level of lover to the level of beginner, *mubtadi*ʿ. This book then elaborates nine steps which will take him to the first stage of discipleship, *mustaʿid,* and from there will take him to the level of full discipleship, *murīd*.

When the seeker reaches the levels of a full disciple, he begins to receive ever more heavenly understanding, which will raise him through three Circles of Certainty. First it will take him to Certainty of Knowledge, *ʿIlmu 'l-Yaqīn*; then to Certainty of Vision, *ʿAynu 'l-Yaqīn*; and finally he will reach the Reality of Certainty, *Ḥaqqu 'l-Yaqīn*. Thus, he ends up in the level of reality.

As soon as the seeker begins to ascend the nine stages, taking him from beginner to disciple, he begins to develop the Knowledge of Certainty and its effects begin to appear to him and in him. At that time, the veils begin to be removed. First he will receive the Power of Hearing; followed by the Power of Seeing and finally the Power of Experiencing Reality.

He moves from level of audio to the level of video, and then from analog to digital. This allows him to receive more knowledge in ever-increasing amounts. It will be as if he is living the past, present and future. He will be hearing, seeing and experiencing what others have gone through, as revealed to him by his master. It will not be like hearing someone tell him a story, rather, in these stages he will actually be living that story, as if he is part of it. He will not simply be viewing events, but will actually take part in them, beginning to feel and sense all that the actual participants did. This is a higher level. He will begin to feel with the people he meets just as if he is one of those present in that person's past. That is the first step to becoming, not just someone who is learning, but someone able to give knowledge and help others. It is also the first level of a spiritual healer. That is why the healer can feel and sense with the patient, and for that reason he is able to powerfully support those who are ill, whether spiritually or physically.

As he inherits spiritual abilities from his mentor, someone who has previously mastered the Way, the disciple will begin to have the power to sense and experience the lives of others. If they are experiencing difficulties, suffering depression or feeling spiritually uplifted, he will feel it. He becomes part of them, so he knows what they need. This will allow him to build others. As well, it will lift him up to reach the level of the six realities of the heart described in the final section of the book, at which time the seeker has advanced from beginner, *mubtadiʿ*, to initiate, *mustaʿid*, and has arrived at the level of disciple, *murīd*.

INTRODUCTION TO THE NINE STEPS: FROM INITIATION TO DIVINE SUPPORT

Before we begin we have to realize that God said in Holy Qur'an:

> *Obey God, obey His Prophet and His Messenger, and obey those in authority among you."*[4]

Obey the law of your country. God is Sultan of sultans, King of kings. He is not like the kings of this world and He is more than the king of this universe. If we say "God is the Sultan" or "Sultan of sultans," and we think in our mind that He is <u>in</u> this creation as a Sultan, then that is *shirk.*[5] He cannot be compared to His creation. God is independent of creation. Creation is dependent on God.

When God says, "Be," things come into existence. The word for "be" in Arabic is "*kun*." Before He finishes saying the word "*kun*" – between the first and last letter— creation comes into existence according to His Will. His Will caused our creation to appear for the sake of *Sayyīdinā* Muhammad ﷺ, His beloved prophet and servant, whom God Himself described as the Messenger of God ﷺ.

The reality of the Prophet Muhammad ﷺ being a messenger is fundamentally tied to Allah's lordship. The existence of the servant is always in relation to his Lord. The Prophet ﷺ is

---

[4] Sūratu 'n-Nisā (Women), 4:59.

[5] Arabic: *shirk*: associating partners with God; idolatry, the worst form of unbelief.

dependent on God—his name always has to follow the Creator's Name. For that reason, the words "Muhammad is the Messenger of God" ﷺ always follow, in complete submission, to "There is no God but Allah" in the profession of faith.[6] In order to approach an understanding of God's Lordship, we have to approach it through the Messenger ﷺ. The fact of their being attached to one another and the fact of this requirement of going through *Sayyīdinā* Muhammad ﷺ to reach God is shown even in the binary nature of the statement of faith: "There is no God but God, and Muhammad is His Messenger." There is no way other than through the Prophet ﷺ. It was the Prophet ﷺ who came and taught "There is no God but Allah."

God said in Holy Qur'an,

> *It is no virtue if ye enter your houses from the back: It is virtue if ye fear Allah. Enter houses through the proper doors: And fear Allah. That ye may prosper.*[7]

What is the door to our Creator? It is not correct to say, as some do today, that "There is no door." If there is no door, why do we affirm "Muhammad is the Messenger of God" after first affirming, "There is no God but God"? If there were no door it would be enough to say the portion of the profession of faith relating only to God.

Islam is not Islam without the portion that relates to the Prophet ﷺ, because like us, Christians and Jews believe that there is no god except God. They agree that there is a Creator. What differentiates us as believers in Islam is that we say, "Muhammad is the Messenger of God." He is the door to God's Lordship.

---

[6] Arabic: *Lā ilāha illa-Llāh Muḥammadun rasūlullāh*: there is no god except the one God, Allah, and Muhammad is the prophet of Allah.
[7] Sūratu 'l-Baqara (the Heifer), 2:189.

There is no other way other than to say, "Muhammad is the Messenger of God" ﷺ.

A tradition from the Prophet's ﷺ time demonstrates the Prophet's ﷺ is the means of access to God—the tradition of the blind man.

A blind man came to ask *Sayyīdinā* Muhammad ﷺ to see, and the Prophet ﷺ taught him the following supplication:

> Oh God, I am asking You and coming to You, my Lord, through the Prophet of Mercy. O Muhammad, I am seeking the means through you to my Lord.

This shows that *Sayyīdinā* Muhammad ﷺ is the Door to God. That is why the testimony of faith contains one part relating to God and another relating to *Sayyīdinā* Muhammad ﷺ. You are not Muslim unless you say "Muhammad is the Messenger of God ﷺ." It is not enough to only say "There is no god but God."

"Muhammad" and "Messenger of Allah" are a name and a description. Muhammad ﷺ is the name of an essence, and "Messenger of Allah" is a description of that essence. At the same time the attribute of the essence is "the praised one" describing the essence that has been named.

God is dressing that essence with His Divine Gaze—bestowing His endless support and blessings on the essence of *Sayyīdinā* Muhammad ﷺ.

How many names does the Prophet have? 201. But although we may know 201 names, or 500 names, in reality there are infinite names for him because the essence of Muhammad, the Messenger of God ﷺ, describes the whole of creation.

I took a handful of My light and said, "be Muhammad" and from that light I created creation.[8]

God created Muhammad ﷺ first, and from that light He created Creation.

What is the color of this object? Is it white or black? [*Response*: "black!"] No, it is white. How can you prove it is black? I am saying it is white and you are saying it is black.

Because you do not have eyes to see! We do not have the eyes to see whether this is black or white. In your eyes you may see black, but someone else may see it as white. It depends on your perception. Do you not see it as white? White is also going into this object, but white is not being reflected by it. Only black is being reflected by it, but in reality, white is also going in, all colors are passing through it; photons are going through it. It has white, red and blue; it has yellow; it has a rainbow of colors ranging from white to black. You cannot say there is no white in it, although you cannot see it.

Someone with better vision than you may see it as red. There are spots of red that you can see, right? So we cannot say the red does not exist. White also exists in this, but you are not seeing it. If someone has the eyes, the power, the knowledge of vision, he can see that this object is not only black but that it also has all kinds of colors within it.

So how are you going to understand the reality of "Muhammad is the Messenger of God"? Some understand so little that they even say "he came and left, and is finished," may God forgive them and us.

This example shows that saints can understand more than ordinary people—as they dive deeper and deeper into realities,

---

[8] Ibn Jawzī in his *Mawlid al-ʿArūs*.

they can pull out more. Like the Prophet ﷺ—from his essence to his reality, God is adorning him—adorning him endlessly. God is dressing different auras on the Prophet ﷺ.

You have clothes on. They are your clothes but I cannot point at them and say, "This is you." They are only your garments. Your body, which is the real you, is under the clothes. If I want to describe you, I can describe your personality, saying "you are active; you are good; you are generous and so on." The essence or reality is different from the attributes. In just the same way, the different lights that God is adorning the Prophet ﷺ with are separate from his reality.

As God is adorning him with infinite Divine Attributes, we see what emerges; people are understanding Muhammad ﷺ as the description of that essence while this aura, or the granted quality His Lord dressed him with, is separate from that.

If there is a sunny day, you may see the sun's rays outside your window. You may see in those rays very small dust particles floating through the air. By means of the dust you see that there is a ray of sun. The attributes that God is bestowing are like those floating particles. In the same way, you are able to perceive an attribute by means of an essence beyond those attributes (you can see motes of dust by means of the ray of sun). There are other attributes on which no visible ray of sun shines, and therefore you do not see them, but you cannot say they are not there. Everywhere those particles are floating, appearances that you cannot see without the rays of the sun. The sun is the source of light—rays of energy and light emerge from it, showing you what you could not see without existence of both rays and particles.

You cannot say there are no particles in the air; they are there although you cannot see them. In the same way you may see something as black when in fact it is white to someone who has vision to see. The mercies bestowed on Prophet ﷺ are like these floating particles. As these realities appear, each one is like a floating particle and an entire reality unto itself, everyone is a universe, a galaxy, billions of stars spewing out every second; God is sending these realities on his Beloved ﷺ, who is the essence and symbol of submission.

That is why Muhammad ﷺ always follows Allah in the statement of faith. *Sayyīdinā* Muhammad ﷺ is always in prostration—his essence is prostrating, meaning everything in that essence; all the universes including us, are always in prostration, never raising their heads, always in submission, always obedient to their Lord. Never is the spirit outside of prostration. It is part of the whole, like a drop in the ocean. The whole that it becomes a part of is the reality behind the phrase "Muhammad is the Messenger of God."

Any part of the whole is related to the whole, like a drop of water—you can take it out of the cup and see it there in your hand; but when you put it back in, it disappears and becomes an indistinguishable part of the whole. So these realities are every moment being dressed from the realities of the phrase "Muhammad is the Messenger of God."

Every moment God is the Creator; this is infinite and cannot stop. As creation is infinite, these appearances are infinite. These realities appear, out of God's creative action, and to all of them Muhammad ﷺ is the messenger. And the essence of the Prophet ﷺ is taking from the Creator, absorbing knowledge as it comes through his essence and that knowledge emerges as appearances—the realities that begin to bring that knowledge forth—whatever realities the essence of the Prophet ﷺ is understanding it gives to these universes.

This is a deep ocean and, Insha-Allah, I will explain that in detail through these lectures. May God forgive us and give us the benefit of tonight, the first night of festival, and God willing, He will bestow upon us the love of His Beloved Muhammad, the Messenger of God ﷺ.

Angels of Answering

Insha-Allah, we will continue discussing the records and manuscripts of Grandshaykh Sharafuddin ad-Daghestani ق, Shaykh Abdullah al-Fa'iz ad-Daghestani ق and Mawlana Shaykh Nazim Adil al-Ḥaqqani ق, may God bless them, *alḥamdulillāh.* God gave saints knowledge that He did not give to anyone else. God gave them a power through which they are able to dig up and bring to light realities from the oceans of knowledge that scholars cannot normally attain. They are taken from the heart of one to the heart of another, and another, and so on... but originally they were taken from the heart of Prophet Muhammad ﷺ.

One of these realties that we are briefly discussing today is that God has created a special kind of angel. How many there are? You cannot count them, they are infinite in number. No one knows their number besides their Creator. Their praising, their *dhikr,* [9] is by only one word that God gave them to say. He gave such angels a specific name, the Angels of Answering, *malā'ikat al-ijābīyūn.*

Grandshaykh is informing us from his visions in seclusion that God said to the Prophet ﷺ:

> I gave you something that I did not give any prophets before you, which no other prophet could carry. I gave it you, especially for you. When I said, *"Lā ilāha illa-Llāh* and *Muḥammadun rasūlullāh"*—from that time until now *"Muḥammadun rasūlullāh"* is following *"Lā ilāha illa-Llāh."* Even before I decided to give you the Holy Qur'an, My ancient Holy Words, I created these angels for the Holy Qur'an. When the Qur'an comes to you and you reveal it

---

[9] Arabic: *dhikr*: any invocation of the Names of God or declaration of sacred phrases (*kalimat ṭayyibah*), inwardly or outwardly, spontaneously or repetitiously, individually or collectively.

to people who then read it, these angels come and repeat "*Amīn*" after every letter. As soon as a person opens the Qur'an and says "*Alif*"[10] the angels say "*Amīn*"[11]. If you say, "*Amīn,* " they say, "*Amīn.*" If you say "*dhālika'l-kitābu...*"[12] they say, "*Amīn, Amīn, Amīn...*"

On every letter of Holy Qur'an I have created different angels for different people who are reading—in every moment a new angel is created whose only job is to say, "*Amīn.*" For every person who reads Holy Qur'an, these angels say "*Amīn*" for every letter, causing that person to be dipped into that letter's ocean of knowledge; God opens the knowledge for the heart of that servant without his awareness. So, for instance, if the reader reads *Sūratu 'l-Fātiḥa,* then for every letter (139 letters, if you include the *Bismi'l-Lāhi 'r-Raḥmāni 'r-Raḥīm* at the beginning) God opens an ocean of knowledge.

From one person to another, the meaning changes and with the meaning also changes that light, that knowledge of each letter in (for example) *Sūratu 'l-Fātiḥa.* Each ocean of knowledge that appears from the letters of Holy Qur'an alters the oceans of knowledge that appeared from the previous letters. The light from each letter for which they say "*Amīn*" will appear for that person on the Day of Judgment. If a person is trying his best to read Holy Qur'an and makes 9 mistakes out of 10, with only one word correct, then God sends these angels and makes them recite the Qur'an correctly, so that He can disburse the rewards given to the servant who reads it correctly—thus He rewards the servant and opens that knowledge for his heart.

---

[10] The first letter of the Arabic alphabet and also the first "word" of Qur'an after Sūratu 'l-Fātiḥa, in a verse comprised of three Arabic letters. (Sūratu 'l-Baqara (the Heifer), 2:1) The entire verse is "*Alif Lam Mim.*"

[11] Arabic: *Amīn*: Amen, "May God accept."

[12] "*This is the book...*" (Sūratu 'l-Baqara (the Heifer), 2:2). The entire verse is: "*This is the Book: in it is guidance, without doubt, for those who fear Allah.*"

God sends them, and they descend on every person that recites the Holy Qur'an until he completes his reading. When someone completes the Holy Qur'an from beginning to end, God sends 72,000 angels. When that servant finishes reading, God will accept his supplication, even if he made mistakes—still these 72,000 angels correct the mistakes and say, "*Amīn*." Even if he makes mistakes on 9 out of 10, God sends those 72,000 angels to correct them.

There is a hadith of Prophet ﷺ "My community is going to separate into 70 or more different divisions."[13] Other hadith speak of 73 divisions, with one of them being safe. The other 72 divisions are not safe.

In another *hadith* the Prophet Muhammad ﷺ said, "The whole Muslim community is like one body."[14] These two hadith in combination mean that the structure of a body and form is going to divide itself into 73 divisions, 72 of which obey bad desires, while one side is saying "Be good, be good, be good."

Even every self is going to divide.

That is why when you recite Qur'an, God sends 72,000 angels to say, "*Amīn*" to correct the other 72 ways that are going astray. For every one of the bad desires, God sends 1,000 angels. That is why the total number of angels coming to help you equals 72,000.

They say, "*Amīn*," God accepts because these angels are saying "*Amīn*." That is why they are called the Angels of Answering, *malā'ikat al-ijābiyūn*.

It is very important to make supplication at the end of the Qur'an because God has sent it to His Prophet ﷺ to make His Prophet ﷺ great. The greatness of the Holy Qur'an is shown when

---

[13] Related in similar wording by al-Ḥākim, Tirmidhī, Ibn Hibbān, Abū Dāwūd, *ṣaḥīḥ*.

[14] Bukhari and Muslim.

these angels come to make supplication. Grandshaykh says the bodies of these angels are soft and subtle, not like ours. God makes His angels great. Their form is so subtle that 700,000 can stand in the place of a finger and yet there is room for all of them to stand there. God makes them very tall because like the *muezzins,* on the Day of Judgment, they call *adhān*. They say "*Amīn*" higher than any person does on the Day of Resurrection. From their height they have a vista of 50 years. From that height they are saying "*Amīn*" and reciting responses for the person who is reciting Qur'an.

There are two kinds of knowledge. One kind is dim, devoid of light. It is like this light, if you turn this off you cannot see. Turn this off. Ah, what happened? It is dark. There is a difference—that light is like people who are studying Latin, or are lecturing in schools and universities. Because they lecture and do not practice there is no light coming from their lectures.

A "spotlight" is like someone who is taking his knowledge from a continuous source of enlightenment and energy, a source that is always shining. Like the sun, it does not reflect light, rather it is a source of light. So this is a source of light, a spotlight.

God described the sun as a source of light, *ḍiyā*. There is a big difference between a source of light and a reflector of light. God mentions in Holy Qur'an that *ḍiyā* is a source of light and that *nur* is a reflection of light. The sun, the source of light, makes people want to go outside so that they can move with its energy. Without the sun's energy, everything would die.

God has given His Prophet Muhammad ﷺ as a source of energy, a source of light that shines on this universe. God made *Sayyīdinā* Muhammad's ﷺ name from four letters, *Mīm, Ḥā, Mīm, Dāl*. And God brought the name Muhammad after His own name, because He ordered the Pen to write "*Lā ilāha illa-Llāh Muḥammadun rasūlullāh.*" You say "*There is no God but Allah*" and directly afterwards you say, "*Muhammad is the Messenger of God.*"

When we say, "He is God, King of kings," it means He is the Creator above whom there is no other creator—the Creator is the reality which is pointed to by *Lā ilāha illa-Llāh.*

Don't listen to me, listen to the one who is speaking in me now—this is not in a book, it is directly from the heart of my Shaykh and from the heart of his Grandshaykh's heart and a whole lineage of saints, prophets, and shaykhs, directly back to the heart of our Prophet ﷺ. They know we are weak and cannot do what they ask us to do. People are happy with candy; if you give candy to children they will be happy; in fact everyone is happy with candy. They do not understand that these are diamonds; regardless, saints give diamonds to the hearts of their spiritual children.

Regardless of the students' weaknesses and sins, God bestows His mercy on everyone. This meeting just now is a meeting in the presence of the saints of God. They are looking at us from that light. We cannot understand, cannot see, we can only learn letters and not understand what is behind those letters. Those whose mindset is to look only at materialistic issues are unable to see this light. We are not able to understand the reality of the spotlight with which you can see everything around you.

Scientists are unable to understand without seeking, experimentation and discovery. Some 500 years ago, scientists came to a great scholar of their time—he was a gnostic from Egypt. They asked him, "Describe for us the difference between external knowledge and internal knowledge."

He looked around and said:

> The question you are asking shows me you do not know anything. You are asking about external knowledge and internal knowledge, but for us there is no internal knowledge; it is all external. We have a spotlight with which we can see everything. It is a reality. You cannot

see in the darkness—you think that everything exists, but for you it is not a reality that everything exists. You might think that anything you cannot see does not exist.

If there is an ant here it can see whether something is bread or rice. We cannot see that with our eyes, but ants can detect it. An eagle can see its prey from high above, from the sky to the ground, and can come and take it and eat it. For us in comparison to you it is as though we had eagles' eyes. We can sense what you cannot sense. We can feel what you cannot feel. We can move where you cannot move, we can talk where you cannot talk.

And this is as the hadith of Prophet ﷺ:

My servant approaches me through voluntary worship until I love him; when I love him I will be his ears that he can hear with, I will be his eyes that he can see with, his ears that he can hear with, I will be his tongue can he can talk with, I will be with hand that he can touch with, and I will be his feet that he can walk with.[15]

Scientists are helpless and cannot describe anything. They say this universe came out of a big bang—that there was a big explosion and that everything came out from this. Well, let us go along with them and agree for the sake of discussion that this creation did come out of a big bang. A big explosion came out and everything was moving in space. We know that today everything in this universe is in a vacuum and in a vacuum there is no gravity, no repelling force, so when that big bang came and this explosion happened, everything came violently outward and there was no repelling counterforce to stop the driven particle. They should have moved outward forever.

---

[15] Bukhari.

I am not going to go deeply into that subject. I will cut it here, but we would like to say that scientists do not understand until they discover things—but saints have the eyes to see far more than scientists can see. Who stopped these particles at the correct moment and kept them tight with a force opposite to the one with which they were originally moving? One force was coming from one side and another force was stopping that movement. Physicists should understand this question. Galaxies, all of them, are not hitting each other. They found billions of galaxies with the Hubble telescope—there are billions of galaxies that are beyond the far edge of the universe, all of which have billions of stars and all the stars in their positions. All of these creations are outside the reality of "*Lā ilāha illa-Llāh*" because they are in the creation, which is beyond his Oneness. Actually they are in the reality of "Muhammad is the Messenger of God" ﷺ. Outside the level of Oneness, everything created is outside the Creator.

Who is outside that? *Muhammad is the Messenger of God* ﷺ is the creation. The creation cannot be in, it has to be out. Who is out? Muhammad ﷺ is the representative of the creation. Immediately after *Lā ilāha illa-Llāh* are the four letters of Muhammad ﷺ. The name "Muhammad" alone has no meaning, but "Muhammad is the Messenger of God ﷺ" has meaning. He is outside of the Creator; he is the Messenger of all creation.

How many universes are there other than this one? And that is why God created this one *Muhammad the Messenger of God* ﷺ—as that of praising God.

"To whom belongs the kingdom this Day?"[16] God said in Holy Qur'an that He is Owner of the kingdom. *Mulk* means kingdom, *Malik al-mulk*—the Owner of the kingdom, is God.

---

[16]Sūratu 'l-Ghāfir (the Forgiver), 40:16.

Everything in this universe has a mass, a structure of protons and neutrons. Every mineral, every element in the periodic table, has a mass within which are protons. Everything outside the Creator has both mass and energy, in the form of light. Every atom has a light, and its electrons are spinning counter-clockwise in the same direction that we are circumambulating the Kaʿbah. Everything in existence is making *dhikr* and praising God. If that *dhikr* disappears, everything disappears. Everything appears in the universe under the name of "Muhammad is the Messenger of God" because *Sayyīdinā* Muhammad ﷺ is the secret and the reality of the creations that God created.

You have to know that God said in Holy Qur'an that Muhammad ﷺ is "in you."

> *A similar (favor have ye already received) in that We have sent within you a Messenger of your own, rehearsing to you Our Signs, and sanctifying you, and instructing you in Scripture and Wisdom, and in new knowledge.*[17]

We are from body <u>and</u> from light; everything in creation has mass and energy. In Arabic, *dunyā* is the mass, *ḥayāt*[18] is the spirit. *Dunyā* and *ḥayāt* come from the secret of the atom of *Muḥammadun rasūlullāh*, and that is why his name is from the four letters *Mīm, Ḥā, Mīm, Dāl.*

Mīm, Ḥā the first two letters, is for *Malik al-Ḥayāt,* the King of Life; *Mīm Dāl* is for *Malik ud-Dunyā,* the King of this world. He is the owner of this world and the owner of life. God gave to Muhammad ﷺ these two special gifts and God owns Muhammad ﷺ, who is dependent on following Him. That reality is enough for us for our whole life, here and hereafter. That secret

---

[17] Sūratu 'l-Baqara (the Heifer), 2:151. See also, 3:101, 49:7.

[18] The principle meaning and usual translation of *dunyā* is "this world." *Ḥayy* is normally translated as "living," and *al-Ḥayy,* the Ever-Living One, is also the 63rd of the 99 Names of God.

is being given from our shaykh—knowledge that is opening just now. Every moment, God is sending secret knowledge to His saints, to their hearts. If you obey God, God supports you. If you obey the Prophet ﷺ, then the Prophet ﷺ will support you. If you obey those in authority, they will support you.

Grandshaykh says, "If you disobey God, there is a way of repentance, if you disobey Prophet ﷺ, there is a way of repentance. But if you disobey those in authority, they throw you to prison, you are finished."

The Prophet ﷺ sends mercy to humans. Allah said, on the tongue of the Prophet ﷺ, "My mercy has overridden My anger."[19]

If you disobey leaders it means you are in big problems. Leaders have no mercy. They have no tolerance, they do not accept any mistakes.

God is the owner of the Chair,
Muhammad ﷺ, the Messenger of God
is sitting on that Chair.
Leaders do not know
how they got their chairs.

A Rope, an Axe, and a Night in a Grave

A wealthy man died, and before he died he asked that somebody go into the grave with him to accompany him through his first night in this new dimension.

At that time, they used to make graves underground spacious, like rooms. The people burying the man who died looked through the whole village to see who would go with that saint and stay with him in his grave. They looked, but no one would go.

[19] Bukhari.

Who can do that? If you go to the graveyard in the evening you will be afraid. Who will go there and sit until morning? Finally they found an old man who bargained on the price, because he was in need of money. They said they would pay him in the morning when they opened the grave.

The old man was a wood cutter who cut wood in the forest. He had an axe and a rope, and that was all he owned. He did not own any airplanes. He was not a pilot. He was not an owner of high buildings. He owned only a rope and an axe.

He went down and they closed the grave. When everyone left and they closed the grave, who comes but two angels, Munkar and Nakīr. They are the Angels of Questioning and will ask everyone in the grave these questions, "Who is your prophet?" "What is your religion?" "In whom do you believe?"

Now since there was this live person there, they saw he was sitting there and they decided to question him instead of the dead person, for they could leave him till later. So they began. From evening to morning they were asking him: "how did you get that rope? How much did you buy the rope for? What did you cut with the axe? Do you hurt the trees when you cut with the axe? Do you harm the environment when you cuts the trees?"

Until morning they were asking him questions and he did not know what to answer, and that was for a simple rope and an axe. The morning came, and he was very happy when they opened the grave, and he ran away.

They said, "Come get your money!" He said, "For a rope and axe they asked me so many questions. If I take the money, how will I answer for that?"

How are we going to answer for the huge number of plates of food we are eating? How are we going to answer?

That is why when the Sultan Hārūn ar-Rashīd asked his brother Bahlūl to come live with him in the palace, Bahlūl said,

"No. Every day I am milking my goat—that is it. That is all I am eating. If God asks me about all the food that is going through the palace, how am I going to answer?"

Give in God's way and God will forgive us. He grants us the holy status (*baraka*) of this night.

Bahlul's House in Paradise

You heard about Bahlūl. He was the brother of the King of Baghdad, Hārūn ar-Rashīd, who was very rich and strong. Not now, a long time ago. Now there is no such king anymore. Now all leaders are dictators.

Bahlūl had memorized the whole Qur'an. He had not memorized it as people today who say "we are *ḥuffāẓ*."[20] At that time, if someone memorized the Qur'an, he knew why it was revealed, what was the story behind each verse's revelation, what was the issue about which each verse was revealed, and what *hadith* support each verse.

He was a very good king, not like today. Leaders of today have no mercy in their hearts. Hārūn ar-Rashīd had a wife who was coming back to the palace after a journey. Bahlūl was sitting and playing with the king's children. Hārūn ar-Rashīd saw his brother and said, "Come sit with me on the throne. Come sit with me and you can call yourself the minister, viceregent, president or regional director—whatever, any title you want, I will give you. Come!"

Bahlūl said, "I am happy here."

Satan plays with us. When you know you are on the right way, you balance yourself, and whether someone praises you or curses you with the worst of curses it does not change you. It is as if nothing happened. You are far from this level when someone

[20] Arabic: *ḥuffāẓ*: People who memorized the entire Qur'an. (Singular, *ḥāfiẓ*.)

tells you, "*Mashā-Allah*, you are like a big lion," and you become very happy. Then when someone tells you "You are a donkey" you become sad. Lions and donkeys are both animals. You are a human being, and better than them.

You will not take with you any more than what you could eat or wear, everything more than that you will leave behind. You may have 10 million in the bank, yet you can take none of it with you. What you take with you is your reputation.

Bahlūl said, "No, I am happy here." Hārūn ar-Rashīd asked him, "What are you so busy doing?"

"I am the builder, the contractor of small sticks," and he had built many houses out of sticks. Rashīd asked, "Can I have one?" "Yes," Bahlūl said, "but for a price." "How much?" "One silver coin."

"It is expensive. All these sticks here—it is nothing."

"If you want one, one silver coin, if you do not want, fine."

His wife said, "No, no, Bahlūl, I will buy one, do not listen to my husband, I will buy one."

That night the king and queen slept, and they both saw the same dream. When they woke up the queen began telling her husband her dream, which of course was the same as his. They saw Bahlūl was building palaces in Paradise, and one of those palaces had her name on it, Zubaydah. It said, "This is your palace, go there and stay. You are being sent to Paradise and this is your palace forever."

Hārūn saw the palace of his wife and it said, "No, you cannot enter, this is the palace of your wife." He saw his brother outside the next day, playing with the children and the sticks, and said," I want one palace. How much?"

"10,000 golden coins!"

"What! Yesterday you said one silver coin! Today you say 10,000 golden coins? What is this? Is there no mercy in your heart?"

"This is my price, if you want it, take it. Otherwise fire is waiting for you. O my brother, do you not know that when archangel Gabriel ﷺ asked Prophet Muhammad ﷺ about the five prayers of Islam, and faith, and the Prophet ﷺ said that you have to believe in the unseen? I told you and you did not believe me until you saw the dream. So now the price is higher."

All of Islam is built on the Unseen, *ghayb*. When you see it, it is finished. Give God a beautiful loan and He will increase it for you. If you give in God's way, God will give that money in the afterlife. If you do not give, God does not give you.

"O my brother, if you want to pay 10,000, that is okay. If you say one word more it will be 100,000 instead."

So the king said to his minister, "Get my brother 10,000 gold coins. He seems to love this world so much." He forgot he is the rich king with so much wealth, and he wanted to see what Bahlūl would do with the 10,000 gold coins.

He sent the army to see what Bahlūl would do with the 10,000 coins. At night, they followed Bahlūl as he went into very old alleys, small roads behind homes. What was he doing? He was throwing all the coins into people's homes.

After he heard this, Hārūn ar-Rashīd sent his guards to all these homes to find out who they were. What did they find? All the homes were those of orphans and widows.

Hārūn ar-Rashīd then went to his brother and said, "O, my brother, you are better than me. I thought you were only playing with the children and playing with sticks. Come be the king and sit on the throne. I will resign."

And Bahlūl said, "No, I am happy with what I have."

Always, even if they have all the money of the world, such people are not affected in their hearts. Regular people, if they are given millions, become so happy that they shake—one might have a stroke on hearing such news! People today are leaving everything and going to seek presidents and kings. What do they take with them when they die? Who was richer than the emperor of Persia? He was one of the richest in the world. What did he take with him?

Mawlana was so amazed when he was traveling in Indonesia through all these villages, and he saw so many old people, eating a little bit of rice and happy with their life. If you are poor and happy with your Lord, you will be happy with a little bit of rice. If you are rich but yet unhappy with your Lord, then even if you own all of this world, you will not be happy.

"Thankful rich"[21] means a rich person to whom God gave money, and he gave it in the way of God. He can build and help hundreds of thousands of orphans and students. God likes that. Worshipping and giving in the way of God is better than being poor, doing all your prayers and having nothing to give.

God said, "Those who waste their money are the brothers of Satan."[22] May God forgive us and grant us the *baraka* of this life. And God's Prophet ﷺ said, "Never does money run short from charity."

"Obey God, obey Prophet, and obey those in authority on you."[23]

I have only created Jinn and men, that they may serve Me.[24]

---

[21] Arabic: *ghanīyyun shākir*: a wealthy person who is grateful for what he has.
[22] Sūratu ' l-'Arāf (the Heights), 7:201.
[23] Sūratu 'n-Nisā (Women), 4:59.
[24] Sūratu 'dh-Dhārīyāt (the Winds that Scatter), 51:56.

"Only to worship Me" has many meanings. Everything you do in this world, if done in God's way, if done according to Shariʿah, is considered worship. If you keep Shariʿah, that is considered worship. Even in breathing; if you fail to remember God when inhaling and exhaling, that means that you are not at that moment in full worship. Everything you do, even breathing, must be done remembering God. You work. You remember God and say, "I am doing this in His way to raise my children in an Islamic way, to help in supporting Islam, building hospitals and schools, and not to going to night clubs."

For everything God established discipline. You have a job; that is discipline in your life. The Naqshbandi *ṭarīqah* has discipline. If you do not follow discipline, you are out of *ṭarīqah*.

The highest manner of discipline is what you follow in order that you will be considered a follower of the Naqshbandi *ṭarīqah*. In general, the highest manner of discipline in *ṭarīqah* is to keep everything in the highest way that Prophet ﷺ mentioned in Shariʿah. The best of good manners is to keep the highest discipline in *ṭarīqah*; if a follower wants to be a follower, he has to accept all the courtesy of *ṭarīqah*, he must follow them all one by one.

He must follow the external meaning and the internal meaning. The Prophet ﷺ mentioned in Shariʿah that we must follow without leaving one *sunnah* behind. The real meaning of manners is that in addition to following the discipline of Shariʿah, he must note and see what is happening, must continue his every breath, both its inhaling and exhaling, without being heedless of remembering God.

The real meaning of the discipline in the Naqshbandi *Ṭarīqat* is that the follower must remember, note, and see all his breaths, his inhaling and exhaling, remembering God in every breath, with every cell of his body. He must absorb all, remembering with every cell of his body. He must not be heedless. With more than three trillion cells, he must make sure that every single cell is remembering God.

You must keep an eye on your body always, and keep remembering God in your heart. We know there are trillions of cells in the body, but you have to keep an eye on your body and ensure that all these cells are praising and remembering God. Expend all your powers, external, internal, physical and spiritual energy, in the way that God has said to spend them. The servant has to recall for what God created him on the Day of Promises,[25] and he must follow that. He has to know why God created every cell of his body, every organ, every sinew, every muscle, every bone, every part of his body—and what is the secret behind each one's creation. This is in order to worship correctly. And that is the lowest discipline of *ṭarīqah*.

Life is not only to wake up every day, look in the mirror and say, "O I look nice, I will wear these new clothes." It is not to look handsome every day and go, saying, "I have to marry this girl because she dresses nicely." The mind is always seeking to look nice, but in *ṭarīqah*, you have to know how to look nice in the Divine Presence of God.

"Come to Me, O My servant, with the best of worship! Don't come to Me with backbiting, only making your clothes nice." Your inner self, your character, must look nice.

---

[25] Arabic: *Yawm al-ʿahdi wa'l-mīthāq*: the Day of Promises, took place in the world of souls, before the creation of mankinds' bodies. Each one of mankind was present at that meeting, and Allah Almighty addressed our souls. God addressed His servants and asked them, "Do you accept Me as your Lord?" Then each soul declared, "Yes, we accept You." All of them declared that He is the Lord and they promised to worship only Him. Further, saints say, each soul accepted the worship that God had written as an obligation for it in the Divine Presence, prior to creation.

Suppose that God collected all of the power of every person on earth, focused it together and gave it to one person who spent it in worshipping his Creator. If such a person worshipped in the highest and best possible way from the beginning to the end of this creation, he cannot reach one drop of the magnificent manners of the Prophet ﷺ. For that reason, saints know that they cannot reach the level of Prophet ﷺ. They are less than prophets and although they spend their entire lives in worship, still they know that what they are doing is nothing compared to Prophet ﷺ. They always feel shy and know that they are less than Prophet ﷺ, and they always ask, "God please forgive us."

They are unable to carry the responsibility, always feeling shy and always in prostration, knowing the meaning of the following verse,

> *We did indeed offer the trust to the Heavens and the Earth and the mountains; but they refused to undertake it, being afraid thereof: but man undertook it; He was indeed unjust and foolish.*[26]

"Heavens" means angels, "Earth" means strong and special people, and "mountains" are saints—and they could not carry it. They all refused that trust. Yet humans beings took it with greediness. They took it and accepted it, and yet failed to keep the trust with discipline. God gave angels the gift of always being in prostration. According to their level they are keeping their worship without for even one instant being absent. Their sustenance is worship.

Prophet Muhammad ﷺ was in worship until his feet were swollen. Saints are always in worship. Everyone took on the Day of Promises what they were able to take and carry of worship.

---

[26] Sūratu 'l-Aḥzāb (the Confederates), 33:72.

While we live in this world we do not follow what we accepted at that time.

In rank, Naqshbandis are the fourth category. The shaykhs will not accept from their followers anything other than the highest level of practice. They will not accept the easy way. You are of a high manner and character. The first level came and this is for Prophet ﷺ. Prophet ﷺ raised his Companions, and they are the second division. His friends and Companions took from his reality. Among them, Abū Bakr aṣ-Ṣiddīq ؓ took from this reality. That place where there is the light to become gnostic.

Then, at the third level, the four imams take from the reality of the Companions. Whatever they have taught of discipline and Shariʿah, they took from the hearts of Companions.

The fourth category is Naqshbandis. They took from the fourth imam *Sayyīdinā* ʿAlī ؓ, and they took from Abū Bakr aṣ-Ṣiddīq ؓ. That is why the Naqshbandi *ṭarīqah* is the most disciplined *ṭarīqah* in this world; from this reality, they accept that God dresses them from this reality. The highest, perfect shaykhs knew the reality of this high manner and character and they asked their followers to follow them.

They characterized their followers in nine levels of worship which, God-willing, we will explain next time.

The description of those nine levels follows in the remainder of this book.

The First Level

These high manners are different from the nine disciplines that were listed as principles of the Naqshbandi Order. These nine, and two more added on, became the eleven that are the basis of the Naqshbandi Order. They comprise the rules of working and behaving in your relationship to your shaykh.

The First Step: Initiation

As soon as the student takes the hand of the shaykh and accepts his guidance, their relationship becomes one of sending and receiving. The shaykh sends and the follower receives. The follower cannot send. The shaykh is like a radio or television, he receives from his shaykh and then relays information to the followers; so it is a continuously open channel of communication, of which the main source is Prophet Muhammad ﷺ. The Prophet ﷺ is sending his inheritance to Abū Bakr Aṣ-Ṣiddīq ﵁, and thereby to the Naqshbandi Sufi Order; from the other side Prophet ﷺ is sending to *Sayyīdinā* ʿAlī ﵁, who also sends to the Naqshbandi Order.

After *Sayyīdinā* Abū Bakr aṣ-Ṣiddīq ﵁ comes *Sayyīdinā* Salmān al-Fārsī ﵁, and then *Sayyīdinā* Qāsim ﵁. Each receives and sends, and the follower only receives. The follower has no power of sending. Only the shaykh is permitted and authorized; and you have accepted to take his hand for his guidance. He can receive and he can send. The follower, again, can only receive.

Not every person will become a shaykh or a guide. Not every person can send and receive. There are only a few saints. They are as rare as diamonds—you cannot find them easily. Not every person assigns himself the caliphate of being able to receive and send. We are speaking of the highest level of saints, those who can receive and send. Others may think that they can receive and send, but they have no power. They are like plastic fruit; they look nice, but they are empty. We saw a lot of such people. In many countries, we see such people—they think they have authority and they have thousands of followers and they keep them, carrying them nowhere, misguiding them. Their responsibility and liability is before God—because they make themselves shaykhs of *ṭarīqah* when in reality they cannot face the fact that they know nothing. That is how mistakes are being made today in all 41 different *ṭarīqats*.

There are three different kinds of shaykhs. Only one of these are real. There are some who make themselves appear as shaykhs or gurus. They go to Baghdad, to *Sayyīdinā* ʿAbdul Qadir Gilani's grave or mosque—there they make themselves shaykhs. They go to Central Asia, to *Sayyīdinā* Bahauddin Naqshband's ق place in Bukhara, Uzbekistan and there they make themselves shaykhs. They go to Egypt or Yemen or India and make themselves shaykhs. These are professional shaykhs, working as such in order to earn money.

The second group is similar. They go to Iraq, Bukhara, Yemen, Egypt, Syria and India and there they study from books, but not from real, living teachers. They may have doctorate degrees in Sufism, but did not learn from real shaykhs. They are shaykhs of books, nothing else. There is no piety with these shaykhs.

The third group consists of shaykhs possessing heavenly knowledge and realities. They are pious people, rare and hard to find. If you find one of them, he is not interested in this world. For him this world is nothing even if he possesses all of its money. He is humble and sits with everyone; he receives from his shaykh's heart and sends to it. He is pious and pure, receiving and sending.

The Second Step: Submission

There was a Naqshbandi shaykh, a real shaykh, who was truly sending and receiving, and he said, "Before I die and you send me to the grave, I am not going to appoint a representative." He said this because normally every shaykh appoints his representative before passing. He knew that he would die; his vision was open. He said, "I am not going to appoint one before I die. Instead you must sit in my masjid and wash my body, but do not bury me until you appoint a representative." They asked, "How will we do that?" He said, "You take my turban down and throw it in the air, and wherever it lands, there will be my representative."

All of his followers gathered as he passed away. All the big people, those who had been to Yemen, India, Bukhara, and Samarkand were sitting there like peacocks and roosters. Too many shaykhs were there! Many were sixty or seventy years of age, although some were young, and all were calling themselves shaykhs according to their knowledge. Generals, ministers, perhaps some kings (because in the earlier times the saints had kings as followers) were present. Everyone was waiting now, anxious for the shaykh to die so they could have his turban.

To real saints, God always grants miracles here and hereafter. They can show miraculous powers to their followers. In the Naqshbandi Sufi Order they must have permission from Prophet ﷺ to show their miracles. In other Sufi Orders they have permission all the time to show such power. In the Naqshbandi *ṭarīqah,* saints do not like to show that power, they prefer to keep it until Judgment Day, hiding their power in order to establish a bond of humanity with their followers. So they keep that power with them, hidden.

The shaykh passed away and they washed his body and put it in a coffin. They went to a big masjid with thousands of people.

Who is going to throw the turban? They began to fight. Each one said "I want to throw it!" "No, I am the older one!" Like this they argued and began to fight over who would throw the turban.

Now the turban is beginning to turn and then everyone takes a stick and tries to make the turban come down on their head. The turban keeps moving and moving and finally there is one person sitting in back, quietly cleaning the shoes and putting them nicely on the rack. The turban went to that person's head.

Prophet Muhammad ﷺ has close ones, but only he has assigned them.

In this way the shaykh showed all his other followers that they were not worthy of receiving the turban. None had reached that humble place of high manners and good discipline except the one far at the back. He would not even open his mouth to say, "Why?" He would sit, and when the shaykh said "Do!" he would completely do what his shaykh asked.

This is the first of the nine manners of *ṭarīqah* that you must carry.

There are shaykhs for money and paper shaykhs. These two groups are not after reality. Reality does not care who is a PhD., who has money. Reality is for those with pure hearts who are in full submission to God. Now they say, "We surrender", although in their hearts they have not really surrendered.

In the time of the shaykh's life, this follower's heart was with his shaykh. The others were shaykhs of letters, sitting in the chair and, *Mashā-Allah,* they were able to speak very nicely, but in their hearts there was no light.

All the way from Prophet Muhammad to Abū Bakr ؓ to *Sayyīdinā* Salman ؓ, all the way through until today, including the entire Naqshbandi Order, there are 39 shaykhs.

Some followers come because they need benefit—the benefit of being around the shaykh, a financial benefit, a worldly benefit, and some want to be representatives. At the same time there are those who come for the love of the shaykh— to be pious and learn.

Those who come for love never say that they are "senior representatives" or claim to be his beloved ones. They are normal people and when they took the hand of the shaykh they entered the first level of good manners. That is, to take initiation from the shaykh, submitting to God's will and understanding that they are submitting to Prophet Muhammad's ﷺ will.

The shaykh has been authorized to take care of them and he understands everything about their lives and will guide them with him. He knows the reality of his follower's mind and the functioning of his spirit, and he can send him information which he will receive. The follower must know that the shaykh knows the smallest reality that the follower has, and every action that the follower does.

Every difficulty that the follower faces, the shaykh is looking at it and watching how he will respond. He has been informed of every difficulty he is facing. The shaykh controls for the follower everything of external knowledge and obligations, and everything of internal knowledge and spiritual powers. The shaykh knows what God has ordered that follower to do in this world through his life. He knows about the Day of Promises. He knows what benefits the follower and what does not benefit him. Therefore the follower must keep submitting to the will of his shaykh.

The shaykh is not going to misguide him or harm him. The shaykh is the receiver from a line going to the Prophet ﷺ, who is the sender. The follower will receive from his shaykh what is needed. He must know that in front of the shaykh he is ignorant (whatever he may think of himself), his knowledge is zero, and that he must not show any knowledge in front of the shaykh. He must know this or he will lose the first of the good manners in the Naqshbandi Order.

The turban went round and round and found that person who was hiding himself, showing humbleness, putting the shoes on the rack. The spiritual symbolism behind "putting the shoes on the rack" is that he never showed his ego or an eagerness to display his knowledge. You must show complete quietness. Don't move in the presence of the shaykh. It is better even if you do not breathe—you cannot do that, but at least be quiet, inside and out.

I am realizing that many times in the presence of Grandshaykh and Shaykh Nazim, if anyone made a noise, that would bring everything down. Your goal is the heart of the shaykh and nothing else. Otherwise you disrupt the shaykh and his connection to his shaykh. Then the light disappears and no more can be transmitted.

Keep Full Presence

Once in the time of Grandshaykh, he was speaking Turkish and Shaykh Nazim was translating into Arabic. There were 500-600 people there and I was sitting there writing and suddenly I scratched my face and Grandshaykh looked at me very strongly to say, "Don't even move! Any of the smallest movements and you disrupt the connection between me and the Prophet ﷺ." And then he stopped talking and left. Any movement of the follower in the presence of the shaykh makes the connection seven times less.

We want complete submission from the follower. Not like a dead person. When you are washing a dead person's hand, he can still tell what is happening although he cannot speak. That is why in Islam it is *ḥarām*, forbidden, to cut the body. Today they perform autopsies, cutting people's bodies. In Islam, you wash the person gently. In the Naqshbandi *ṭarīqah*, you need more submission than that dead body. Instead, be like a dead leaf, which falls without ever complaining.

The dead person will complain, "Be soft with me, wash me gently! Do not crack my bones!" In *ṭarīqah* you must be like a dead leaf. It never complains within, like a dead person. He is feeling everything, but God took his power of speech. Don't say "it is not time." The shaykh knows the wisdom. When your shaykh says to you "Speak," you speak; if your shaykh says to you, "Go," you go. Put your will aside.

Knowing how to read Qur'an—even one letter from Qur'an—takes you to the intercession of the Prophet ﷺ. How many letters are there in Qur'an? 6666! How many letters? Around 500,000 letters. One half of one letter of the Qur'an is better than this whole *dunyā*. Those who do not know how to read it in Arabic are going to regret it and be biting their fingers on Judgment Day. Learn how to read the Qur'an. Do not say, "I read it in another language." Learn Arabic or else you will lose a lot of benefit.

You waste your time at Playstation. You know Playstation. You spend hours at it yet never spend the time to learn how to read the Qur'an.

After the person takes the hand of the shaykh (initiation), he must submit like the dead leaf of a tree, and not like a dead person who still knows what is happening to him. God does not take the whole spirit out of a dead body, but leaves one part there that feels. It senses whether the water is hot or cold, whether he is moved softly or not. However, a dead leaf takes what comes to it without complaining. The follower must not complain; he must surrender to Prophet Muhammad ﷺ and surrender to the wisdom of his shaykh.

Surrender, submit to God's will:

O my Lord, I am surrendering to you, you know about me better. O *Sayyīdinā* Muhammad! You are the messenger of God, you know what is better for me. I am surrendering to you. You are the messenger of God, you know what it better for me.

Step Three: The Right Path

When you surrender to your shaykh, God causes him guide you in the right path. Your surrender immediately leads you to the right path—the way that is always seeking God's pleasure. You are following the way that leads you to the Divine Presence and that will make you a pious person. You have to build up piety and sincerity in yourself.

When you surrender, you say, "He knows better." God knows more than you because He created you and knows what is best for you. You do not have any complaint in front of God's Will, so you have become a very pious and sincere person and you know that "God knows better than me." Therefore you say, "I have to follow this way." If a follower does not surrender, does not submit, does not go to the first level in *ṭarīqah,* then he is going to stay at the bottom of the mountain, going around in circles, never going up.

People who do not surrender are always complaining. They are always busy in this life, and this makes them slaves of worldliness rather than slaves of God. When you surrender to God, you will be following His order.

Allah taught us to pray, in every *rakaʿat* of the five daily prayers and in every sunnah prayer:

Guide us to the straight path.[27]

The straight path is the one with no zigzags, no wandering, no side trips and no distractions. A school child knows that the shortest distance between two points is a straight line. Just as a

[27] Sūratu 'l-Fātiḥa (the Opening), 1:6.

zigzag pattern of travel creates a longer physical trip, so a meandering spiritual journey stretches out the distance to the goal. If you have embarked on the Path of Surrender, Satan's primary power over you is to misdirect you and lead you off the path, at least temporarily. You will still reach the goal, but the journey is extended.

If you are under the *bayaʿ* of a shaykh, he has the duty to bring you there, but it takes longer. As you waver on the path it creates vibrations that are detectable by your shaykh. That is why it's best not to ask, "Why I am not receiving my Trust, *amānāt*?" The reason is that your journey is becoming longer because, strictly speaking, you are not taking *ṣirāṭ al-mustaqīm*—the straight path. That is the mode of travel for people who kept their covenant with God, the Exalted. They are always straightforward.

Step Four: *Taqwa*

The Prophet ﷺ said:

> There is in the body a piece of flesh, and if that small flesh is good the whole body is good and if this is corrupted then the whole body is corrupted and this is the heart.

To fix the heart you need sincerity, piety. If there is no sincerity, and piety, and *taqwā* is to know that Allah ﷻ is always watching you, then you are not going to reach perfection.

There are many people they claim that they want to teach others. They give themselves titles. Professors or psychologists or shaykhs or gurus or masters or psychiatrists, or whatever they may be, but already their heart is malfunctioning and there is no sincerity and no piety.

The heart is like a bird in a cage. To fix the heart needs *taqwā*—piety. What is *taqwā*. Consciousness. To always be watching yourself, because Allah is watching you.

Awliyāullāh they fixed their hearts. They didn't sit on chairs to give guidance until they perfected themselves. First they have to give irshad to themselves. If there is still something left they must perfect themselves.

Our Grandshaykh said:

> O Muslims! You are in need when you are alone wrong you have to keep that belief that Allah is seeing you so that you don't do something wrong. And you have to come against the four enemies: ego (*nafs*), love of this world (*dunyā*), lustful desire (*hawā*) and Satan. Don't give anything that your self is asking. Don't give what your lustful desires are asking. Don't give what your love for *dunyā* is asking. Don't give in to what Shaytan is asking. Give what Allah is asking.

Step Five: Divine Support

Our Grandshaykh relates:

> Prophet Muhammad ﷺ called the Companions early one morning at sunrise and said, "Come to Mount Uḥud." When they were there, he said, "The sun is rising, give your back to the sun and look at the mountain."

So when the sun was at their backs, their shadows were in front of them. He said, "Run after your shadow!" Since they were facing West, the sun was behind them and they could never catch the shadow; it was always ahead of them. They could not catch it but they ran all the way to Uḥud.

So Prophet ﷺ shouted, "Look at me now!" They looked at him facing East towards the rising sun. He said, "Run to me now!" When they reached him, he said:

> O my Companions, whoever comes to me, looking toward the afterlife, looking toward God's way, God makes this world chase after him like your shadows

> chased after you. As fast as the shadow is running after you, that is how fast this world is chasing you. It will run after you. But if someone runs from me and goes after worldly things, like when you were chasing your shadows, God makes them run after them and become slaves to worldliness like people vainly chasing their own shadows.

So submit to the wisdom of the shaykh, and he guides you. When he guides you on the right path you begin to become pious. First comes initiation, then you reach the level of submission; when you reach the level of submission that takes you to the straight path. Those who are on the straight path come to the level of the Station of Piety. When you reach the Station of Piety, you go from there until you reach the Station of Divine Support, and God gives you support.

These five steps together comprise the first step of the good manners of the Naqshbandi *ṭarīqah*.

The Second Level—Your Daily Personal Liturgy

Prescription to Atomize

What you have to build on top of the first step is what the shaykh prescribes for you as medicine to cure yourself. Everyone is sick. We are all sick. We need a doctor, a spiritual healer,[28] but what is necessary is a real spiritual doctor, not one whose main concern is money, and not one whose knowledge is from paper—dry and untrained.[29] You need a real spiritual healer, one of the spiritual healers from the Prophet ﷺ.

So the shaykh knows that you are sick and he looks into your heart like a doctor and checks it. The doctor takes a stethoscope and looks at your heart, how many beats it is beating. If it is alright, he says so; and if it is not then he will give you some medicine. With the stethoscope, the doctor can quickly find the problem if the problem is acute, but if the problem is more chronic he goes to a bigger machine, an EKG machine. On the graph that is generated, the doctor reads all the waves that show the problem with the heart.

---

[28] Called a *ḥākim* (wise person) or *ḥabīb* (loved person).

[29] In Egypt there is one spiritual healer who shows the dangers of false healers; he married 70 women. Be careful. God gave permission to do some things, and when God gives permission no one can stop it. God gave permission for men to marry four women, but there are conditions, disciplines and laws for that: and not everyone can carry that responsibility. It is not correct to marry a woman only to divorce her, then take another woman in marriage and divorce her. It is a sunnah of the Prophet ﷺ to marry more than one wife, but you must satisfy God's conditions for that. It is not the correct way, as you see it done today, that people around the world marry and divorce repeatedly. Don't be like that.

Many people are sick in their hearts, not physically but spiritually. The shaykh knows everyone is sick, so as a first step he can give a medicine that is good for you. There is a disease that everyone has, so the shaykh immediately says, "This is your medicine, take it!"

Sometimes you go to the doctor and you have pain, and he puts the stethoscope on your chest and says "there is nothing." But you say you feel pain, so he goes to the EKG machine. With the EKG, he checks inside, and still does not find anything. He may say there is nothing, then put you on an isotope machine to expose the defects in the heart by throwing atomic particles at it and analyzing the results.

In this way he finds the disease, deep in the heart. He gives you a medication, saying, "Take this morning, noon, evening." Otherwise, he might say, "Take it every six hours," or "take it either in the morning or in the evening." Or he may say, "Take it when you are not eating." Or "Take it after eating." So a different type of medication is taken in different ways.

In the same way, the shaykh knows how deep the disease is. So first of all he gives a normal medication to everyone, then he will say, "All of you recite *Fātiḥa*!" For each person he also finds more in your heart. He now says to a person, "In addition to the *Fātiḥa*, recite (for example) '*Say Allah is One...*'" To a different one he will say, "You recite '*Say I seek refuge with the Lord of the Dawn...*'" To another he might say, "You recite '*Say: I seek refuge with the Lord of men...*'" In this way he gives everyone a different medication.[30]

[30] The four references in this chapter are to, respectively, Sūratu 'l-Fātiḥa, the first chapter of Qur'an, Suratu 'l-Ikhlāṣ, the 112th chapter, Suratu 'l-Falaq, the 113th chapter, and Suratu'n-Nās, the 114th chapter.

He also prescribes a different time of day for each medication. He will say to one to recite his *dhikr* in the morning, another to recite in the evening, he will tell another to recite in the afternoon. The prescribed recitation in its correct time cleanses the person.

So that is how we finish the first step and approach the second step. The shaykhs, through their wisdom, their invocations of praise on the Prophet ﷺ, and through their connection to him, introduce their followers to his presence. From that presentation each person will be prescribed a certain daily personal liturgy (*wird*) that they have to do at certain times of day.

When this happens the follower must keep his daily personal liturgy at the correct times. If not, he will be expelled from the heart of the shaykh, from the presence of the Prophet ﷺ, and from the Presence of God. By failing to keep the daily personal liturgy he is failing to listen to his Shaykh's order, and therefore declining his initiation with the shaykh. He loses his status as a valid follower, and he must then renew his initiation with the shaykh and apologize to the shaykh for leaving the daily personal liturgy.

The preferred times that the saints learn from Prophet ﷺ are:

(1) from one hour before the morning prayer until the sunrise prayer

(2) from the late afternoon prayer to the sunset prayer, and

(3) from the sunset prayer until the night prayer. You have to sit and do the *dhikr* in one of these three times. You can finish them in perhaps one hour. That is it.

If he gave you to say, for example, the statement of faith (*shahādah*), asking for forgiveness (*istighfār*), as usual, and then 1500 "Allah," 100 Praises on the Prophet ﷺ (*ṣalawāt*), it may take 10 or 15 minutes. You have to sit, any time between the time that starts one hour before the pre-dawn prayer until the sunrise prayer—any time! You sit there and do it until it is finished—any time! Or between the sunset prayer and the night prayer, or between the late afternoon prayer and the sunset prayer.

It takes some followers ten minutes to do their daily personal liturgy and then it is finished, and then they can go to work. It takes other followers one hour. Others need two hours. Some need three hours. The amount of time depends on the person and his/her level.

On no soul doth Allah Place a burden greater than it can bear.[31]

God does not burden people except according to what they can carry. *Ṭarīqah* is like this—the shaykh knows how much he is giving you, and how much you can carry and recite every day.

God ordered every human being to keep five obligations. They are well known to you—the statement of faith, prayer, fasting in Ramadan, charity and Hajj. They are the five pillars of Islam. On top of those obligations, the Prophet ﷺ used to practice other worship—therefore, scholars and saints follow these additional practices. They consider these practices obligatory also, because they are the shining footsteps of the Holy Prophet ﷺ.

Saints know what kind of medication each follower needs, because they present their followers to the Prophet ﷺ, and are instructed in giving medication by the Prophet ﷺ.

The follower must keep all the practices of the Prophet ﷺ and his daily personal liturgy. He must keep the daily personal liturgy, every day. He must consider it his obligation because he

[31] Sūratu 'l-Baqara (the Heifer), 2:286. See also, 65:7 (Let the man of means spend according to his means: and the man whose resources are restricted, let him spend according to what Allah has given him. Allah puts no burden on any person beyond what He has given him. After a difficulty, Allah will soon grant relief.)

gave initiation to the shaykh. He must surrender to the shaykh's orders and do the liturgy. If the follower leaves these obligations, he will be cast out of the circle of the saint. The saint is in the Circle of Saints—they are in the circle of Prophet ﷺ, and all of them by Prophet ﷺ are taken to the Presence of God. Therefore by being expelled from the circle of the saint, that follower is also expelled from the presence of all saints and the Prophet ﷺ.

The Prophet ﷺ said, in a *Ḥadith qudsī*:

> Neither My heavens nor My earth contained Me, but the heart of the believer contains Me.[32]

God said this, and it means that God likes to send to the hearts of the believers. It means God sends His Light to the heart of the *wali*. He throws it from the throne of the heart of the saint.

If the follower fails to keep the daily personal liturgy, he is like a patient failing to take his prescribed medication who is then attacked and sickened by many viruses, his whole body deteriorating and falling ill. The follower becomes contaminated, and all kinds of forbidden actions, difficulties and sins will run after him. He is attacked by "viruses." When you fail to do your liturgy, every devil will run after you, destroying your belief, throwing you away from the Presence of God, from the Presence of the Prophet ﷺ, from the company of your Shaykh.

The first level of the heart is where Satan comes and goes. Satan cannot enter the second level—the level of the secret. That is only for saints to enter.

Safeguard Your Heart with the Daily Personal Liturgy

When you are practicing your daily personal liturgy, you are locking the door of your heart so that Satan cannot go in. Failing

---

[32] Al-Ghazālī mentioned it in his *Revival of the Religious Sciences, Iḥyā al-'Ulūm ad-Dīn.*

to do it is like removing the door from your house. Robbers, thieves and smugglers can come in, take everything, and run. In some areas in every country, you can find people who put iron gratings outside of their wooden doors and on their windows. Some people also put another metal door outside their bedroom to keep themselves and their money safe, and then inside that doubly locked room some people, especially women, keep locked safes for their jewelry,

Now, after all that, they might install an alarm system which will call the police station directly if anyone enters. All this means they are alert, 24 hours a day. They are informing the police—"Look, our home is very precious. If anything goes wrong, your company is responsible." If a thief comes in, immediately this alarm goes off, and the police come in.

Our problem is that by leaving the daily personal liturgy we are leaving our doors wide open for Satan to enter, take all our faith, and run away. What is the benefit then of taking initiation with the shaykh? Therefore if you neglect your daily personal liturgy, your shaykh says, "Okay, you are choosing this way? Go by yourself." Still the shaykh is a good shaykh, do not worry! If you do not do the daily personal liturgy, he will do it on your behalf. Mawlana Shaykh Nazim ق will do it for you.

This lesson is about how we must follow; but do not think saints have no mercy in their hearts. Of course they know the followers are weak. So of course they are going to do everything on our behalf, and support us in the Presence of Prophet ﷺ.

More on the Daily Liturgy Prescribed by Your Shaykh

We will continue explaining from the previous session, the importance of keeping the daily personal liturgy. Now we are describing the next step of the characteristics—good manners and discipline of the Naqshbandi *ṭarīqah*.

We said the first step of the ladder was the initiation, and we explained five different things that go with the initiation. Then we said that the second step is the daily personal liturgy, which we must do at the correct times of day, when the shaykh instructs us to do it. Keep this, because it is like medication to heal you from your spiritual sicknesses, according to the wisdom of the shaykh, who learned the daily personal liturgy from the Presence of Prophet ﷺ.

The example of the daily personal liturgy is like a closed door, outside of which there are iron gratings, after establishing which you use an alarm system, connected by telephone to the police so that they are warned of any attempt to enter your house. Failing to do the daily personal liturgy is like having a house with no doors—a thief can easily come and steal everything. Your personal liturgy prevents Satan and his army from entering your heart and destroying everything you have done in your 24 hours of keeping obligations and following the practices of Prophet ﷺ.

Shaykhs look at the hearts and can see the sicknesses of their students. When they see these sicknesses, they must cure them. The shaykhs look at everything that came from Prophet ﷺ, and from that they extract a certain prescription of supplications and Names of God as a remedy for the sickness of the follower. This remedy heals the follower's illness and seals his heart from Satan.

In his lifetime, the Prophet ﷺ mentioned thousands and thousands of supplications. The supplications were not all for general use. Some were for specific Companions, others for other Companions. A Companion might be with the Prophet ﷺ privately—and the Prophet ﷺ might say something that is especially for him, a medication, a reward for that Companion. So that Companion took it for himself, reciting it, perhaps without giving it to other Companions. So that's why we see, in the biography of the Holy Prophet ﷺ, thousands of supplications. Who can read them all? Who can memorize them all? So from these supplications, saints choose what is needed for each person and put it in a certain form, in order to help the person and cure his sickness.

Today, if you have a medicine, they write on it an "expiration date." After that date, do not use it, because it will not affect you. Twenty years ago, the medicine scientists had was definitely less advanced than what we have today, and what exists today can heal better. And possibly the same minerals and elements that they used to use before in a different way, would have a different effect on today's patient. The scientists are not creating something—it already existed, but they are manipulating it in a new way, exposing it to a different reaction or using a different combination, and it yields a different effect on the patient

Today if a patient finds he has cancer (may God protect us from this), and asks a doctor for a medicine that was in use 20 years ago, the doctor will say, "No, I will give you something better that will heal you. Don't take something that is from a different time." This is more advanced, a different 'combination' and with this different combination comes a different reaction from the patient.

The Prophet ﷺ came for all times. So, wise saints are looking at the illnesses of their disciples and applying new combinations of Prophet's ﷺ supplications, his teachings, and giving their students' daily personal liturgies against the diseases of today that did not exist before.

There was no video before! There was no satellite TV before! There was no secular science, as today. There were no politics, like today. There were no pornographic movies, like today. There were no discos, with today's music and big amplifiers, speakers and sound systems. A lot of things never existed before! There were no women on the beaches with bikinis. There were no nude beaches before. Corruption is increasing. Sicknesses, like cancer, are spreading.

Saints are looking at the diseases of the hearts of today's people and applying the teachings of the Prophet ﷺ because he came for all times; and Qur'an is for all times; and the supplications of the Prophet ﷺ are for all times; and the example of the Prophet ﷺ is for all times. Saints take those elements and put them together in different combinations—combinations that cure you or others. Different combinations are for different students. It changes them and has an effect.

Some people say that they are doing their daily personal liturgy, then asking, "Can you show us a little bit of light? Can you show some secrets? A little bit! Not necessary to show us so much!"

Your house, your container, your body, must be strong. The space shuttle, or an airplane, when they go up, must resist the environments in which it flies. If the body of these vehicles were unable to withstand the reactions, forces, speed and heat that are generated during the flight, it would disintegrate. Likewise, our hearts are not yet ready to receive even an atom of light from the light of saints. Your heart would completely explode, and by exploding you would be driven insane—then you will no longer be able to control yourself.

That's why when saints give you a daily personal liturgy, keep doing it—keep doing it and keep doing it. You are strengthening the structural materials of your heart. Making it stronger and stronger and stronger. That way as soon as they begin to give you light inside, it will not crack under the pressure. If it did crack....

Saints do not want to destroy you! They want you to continue, remaining stronger. They do not want you to go crazy. What is the benefit if you go crazy? They want wise people. That's why there are many shaykhs who are not strong enough, in different places, whose followers are crazy. If the shaykh is perfect, he prevents the follower from seeing this Light, to prevent the insanity of the follower.

So what the saints prescribe for you—knowing your sicknesses—do it! Because then you are not wasting your time. You are getting the reward of doing it, and building a solid structure in yourself.

If you do not do it, but rather just do your own home-made personal liturgy, you will still get the reward, because although you will benefit from repeating God's words, you will not be able to solve the problems of your sicknesses; you will not be able to build a solid structure. You do not know what fits you. Saints know. So you might be prescribing for yourself something that is not appropriate for you but that is appropriate for someone else. So do not do other than what the shaykh shows you to do. Don't go to books, and open and read… If you want to read what other shaykhs are saying and doing, it is okay. But finish first what your shaykh has given you of daily personal liturgy. Then go to other books and read whatever you want. At least then you have built your structure and saved yourself.

I see many people carrying a lot of books in their pockets. They are reading and reading... Then why are you taking initiation with your shaykh? To read the books of other shaykhs? Is it not better to do the daily personal liturgy that your shaykh is showing you? If you need more from your shaykh, there is a lot more! You are not asking! The shaykh starts you at the first step. If you have more time to read and you want to read more, and you want to use other supplications, it is okay!

Ask the shaykh, "Can I do more?" He will give you more that might be better for you than going and reading from someone else who does not know you and did not prescribe the supplication especially for you. You'll get the reward if you do that other shaykh's prescription of daily personal liturgy, but you will not get the benefit of medication and treatment.

Not every doctor can prescribe a medication for your sickness! You go first to a general practitioner. He checks you. Then he may say, "I cannot help you, your disease is far beyond my experience." At the beginning he tried to treat you, but then he said, "No, I cannot." He then sends you to a specialist. You go to the specialist, and he says, "Ah, let me check you." Then he says, "We need a consultation." Five or six specialists consult together to see what they can do for the sickness. That is for a very difficult sickness. Then they decide on something that might be 99% correct and effective.

Today there are "professional shaykhs" who make themselves shaykhs in order to collect money. Then there are shaykhs of letters—they can only give dry lectures, they know nothing of realities. And then there are true shaykhs, perfected ones, who are connected with the Prophet ﷺ, and who are pious people; men who kept their vow, who never changed.

Among the Believers are men who have been true to their covenant with Allah. Of them some have completed their vow (to the extreme), and some (still) wait: but they have never changed (their determination) in the least.[33]

Innocent students may look for a shaykh, and may find, by chance, a perfect, pious one. They must thank God if they do. Or, they might find one who is not perfect—they might find a "shaykh of letters," or a "shaykh of money." Those phony shaykhs know that they have no cures for the people visiting them, they cannot prescribe any cure.

But because of their arrogance and pride, and to keep collecting money, they try to cheat their followers, giving them daily personal liturgies that do not work. Instead of being like the general practitioner challenged by a sickness that is beyond his

---

[33] Sūratu 'l-Aḥzāb (the Confederates), 33:23.

knowledge and experience, and who therefore refers his patient to a specialist (a higher shaykh).

The false shaykhs keep the innocent students with them and misguide them. And God is going to misguide those fake shaykhs on Judgment Day. Not misguiding them and sending them to hell. No, because they pray, they do their obligations. But they will not get the highest level with the Prophet ﷺ.

There are also pious people to whom saints have given some specialty, some light to be representatives. They know that they cannot cure followers. They say, "No, we can guide you and direct you to a higher level. Go. That person has the cure for you. Go stay with him and give him initiation." These are good people.

Don't try to prescribe medication for your followers. It might not affect them. Send them to one who is higher and knows what he is giving in order to cure them. And this message is for those shaykhs who are everywhere: If you know that you cannot cure someone, then do not misguide people. Send them on to the real shaykh. They know who is a real shaykh, but do not refer their students, from jealousy and envy and because of their love for position and money (and maybe Rolls-Royces or jet planes).

The disciple of a perfect shaykh has to perform his daily personal liturgy on time. And he has to perform it as the shaykh gave it to him. Without adding or subtracting. It means, do not increase, do not decrease. Do the same number that he gives you.

When you go to the airport, there is a gate that is always closed until the ticketing agent opens it. He or she punches a number and the gate opens. If that number is not correct, the gate will not open! If the shaykh tells you, "Do 5,000 *Allah,*" you have to say 5,000. If you do 5,001, the gate does not open. If you do 4,999, the door does not open. It cannot open! Because it has a code. The Shaykh gave you the code. Why are you not using the code?

There are people now who when they do *dhikr*, do it like this, "Allah, Allah, Allah Allah, Allah...."; speaking quickly, without distinguishing the words. They do not count the repetitions. If the shaykh said to say "Allah" 100 times, then every time you say "Allah" connect and see your heart moving toward the Divine Presence of your Lord, with the company of your Shaykh to the Presence of the Prophet ﷺ; and from the Presence of Prophet ﷺ to the Presence of God. "Allah." You can meditate on it until you begin to dress it completely.

Then it becomes automatic that you say it in the correct way. "Allah. Allah. Allah. Allah." Speaking slowly and meditating on each word. Then you come at the end, and it is 99, then 100. A perfect number. The door opens. But when you say "Allah Allah Allah Allah Allah Allah," quickly, not distinguishing the words, and you finish, look! It is not 100! The door is not going to open! Then you are stuck.

People are doing their daily personal liturgy while watching television now. They sit, turn on the television, or a movie, saying "Allah Allah Allah Allah," quickly, not distinguishing. Or "*Lā ilāha illa-Llāh Lā ilāha illa-Llāh Lā ilāha illa-Llāh Lā ilāha illa-Llāh Lā ilāha illa-Llāh Lā ilāha illa-Llāh.*" Or *ṣalawāt*, like "*Allāhumma ṣalli ʿalā Muḥammadin wa ʿalā āli Muḥammadin wa sallim*" and the television is there and they are looking, watching the news or a movie—everything! Do you see them like that? Is this correct?

So how then are you going to take your medication? How are you going to treat yourself for your sicknesses? The door will not open. It must be done correctly – speaking slowly and carefully "Allah." If you are saying "*Lā ilāha illa-Llāh*", then you have to know that *Lā ilāha illa-Llāh* begins from the belly, taking all these through the seven *laṭā'if*, through seven points of light that are in your chest, moving all these lights toward your right side, saying to your right side the first part: "*Lā ilāha* ("there is no god to be worshipped...") through your whole system, through these different levels that are on your chest – the Naqshbandi levels that have been described, going to the right – "*Lā ilāha*" so getting all this to concentrate the power of all your body through your chest, the seven *laṭā'if,* and then you send it, concentrate it to the right side, and then from there like concentrated laser light, it becomes very small and focused, and then sends it from there to the heart saying "*illa-Llāh*—(There is no god) Except God!" and sending it to the heart. In this way, when you make *dhikr* of *Lā ilāha illa-Llāh,* on the number that the shaykh assigned, then at the last number the door opens: "Come inside. Come to Me." Or else how is it going to come?

If you put pressure on a glass, what will happen? It might crack. What will happen to water in the glass? It will be lost. So with your daily personal liturgy, you have to build yourself—there are more than 3 trillion cells in your body. You have to build a solid system around them, strengthening them, so that if you put pressure on them they will not crack.

And that daily personal liturgy, slowly, slowly, with certain numbers that open gates, move you from one gate to another, from one gate to another, gaining the special aura from each one, because when you open a gate then a special aura comes. You open the second gate, by your daily personal liturgy, and another special aura comes. So you will be dressed with high-strength "metals" or protection; which protection will prevent your body from cracking under pressure.

We must have a container that will not crack like this glass would crack under high pressure. You have to build up a container that can allow and hold high energy or pressure inside.

As God said, "Neither My heavens nor My earth contained Me, but the heart of My believer contains me."

That is a very high special aura, a very high blessing – you have to build a highly resistant container for that special aura when it comes, when God bestows it on you. You have to be able to carry it, or else you will break down completely. Your daily personal liturgy will build up the "pressure capacity" of your body, so that it can hold pressurized "gaseous" contents as some special containers can hold gases like propane or oxygen. In this way all the cells of your body become stronger and stronger and stronger during *dhikr*.

The one that has this state of ecstasy, no one can carry him, even mountains. He will go crazy. So you have to build that kind of heavy structure through your daily personal liturgy so that when permission comes for opening and dressing these special auras, one after the other, you will be able later to be like this perfume container. When I open it, and spray it on, I can smell the perfume.

So the beautiful scent of your daily personal liturgy can only be smelled by yourself, because you are still in liquid form. When you do the daily personal liturgy without "pressurizing" it into a "gaseous" form, its scent does not emanate from you. The effects of your *dhikr* are, metaphorically, still liquid. Only you benefit. It is like a little bit of water in the desert – a small oasis. That is what you can accomplish by making *dhikr* without care as to the number of repetitions you are making. Not more.

But when you continue your daily personal liturgy, opening one door after another by doing it at the right time in the right number (no more, no less) of repetitions, strictly according to your shaykh's instructions, then you open one door, then another, then another, and so on. And these dressings will open for you. Slowly, slowly, those dressings will come over you. So you begin to take it more and more. You build up your structure. Then all your cells are making *dhikr*. Trillions of cells are making *dhikr*, every cell by itself.

With that daily personal liturgy, you progress slowly, from one level to the second, to the third, because you are still not focused, not yet concentrated. But slowly you become able to focus light like a laser or like a magnifier, and the metaphor for that focus is the difference between ordinary sunlight and a beam (of the sun's light and energy) that is focused through a magnifying glass—the focused beam can burn a piece of paper.

In the same way, when you are beginning as a follower and doing the daily personal liturgy, you are still scattered, unable to focus. As you repeat the liturgy, the energy concentrates, concentrates, becomes more pressurized. Under pressure, it comes together. As it comes together more and more, the energy moves from all your cells and concentrates in the heart. And that's why when we say *Lā ilāha illa-Llāh,* the whole body has to say with you, "*Lā ilāha illa-Llāh,*" and imagine that all your cells are saying it, and going to the right side of your chest, on the shoulder, and then coming to the heart saying "*illa-Llah!*" to concentrate, to make that power more concentrated. As it is concentrated and concentrated and concentrated, it becomes a source of light. Under high pressure, that light is concentrated. Then because of the focus and pressure, the effect is not like liquid perfume that affects only those close to the source, but rather like an "atomizer," spreading the smell everywhere when released. As soon as you press it, it sprays perfume throughout the room—everyone in the room can smell it, instead of a liquid perfume that no one can smell except you.

By focusing this energy through *dhikr,* you become a source of beautiful incense for everyone around you. This is, if you are following the right daily personal liturgy at the right time with the right numbers. That is, if you want to become a follower in the Naqshbandi Order. That is, if you want to go to higher and higher levels, and begin to feel something—to feel that you are really accomplishing something.

Many people say, "We have followed this way for seventy years, or eighty years, or twenty years, and we are not seeing anything." Of course you are not seeing anything because you are not following the right way. You are only a 'lover'— you love the shaykh, you come and sit; that is it. You are not yet at the level of manhood. You are still a child. And you can never give a child a diamond! No! Because he does not know its value. So many people are following shaykhs, yet they never see anything. Of course you are not going to see, because you have not raised yourself from the level of childhood to the level of manhood.

As soon as you reach the level of manhood, it is completely different. And that's why now today there are Wahhabis who say "There is no spirituality! There is no Sufism! There are no more saints! Saints are gone!"

Hah! You say they are gone because you are ignorant! You are not seeing them! They are there!

They are not raising themselves to the level of being able to see them! Everything for you is material. Everything for you is physical structure. For you there is no energy. Energy does not exist!

When energy is a secular science, they believe in it—electricity. They will not believe in a religious science of energy! Because they do not believe what they cannot see, and you cannot see energy. Why do you want to see spirituality? You cannot see it, you sense it. You taste it. Energy, you can sense and you can see the effects of its power.

You can see a brain. Its physical structure exists and has mass. And the brain is so huge, yet only one small part of it is the location of intelligence. You cannot see it. You can understand it through the signs of what you do during your life. From those actions we can know how much intelligence you have.

Faith in the unseen is important. If you want to see everything and you do not believe in the unseen – then show me intelligence! Show me the intelligence in your brain. You cannot! I want to see it physically. Can you show it to me? Then if you cannot, you must believe in the unseen.

If they do research and put effort into it, scientists will, at the end of their research, make a discovery. Is that not right? But you have to put all your effort into the research! At the beginning you start with a theory. The theory is not yet correct, just imagination and an assumption—a hypothesis. So you have to try to research it until you discover the truth regarding that thing that you are studying. When you discover it, you are so happy. But by then you have spent maybe 50 years or 70 years of your life!

So how do Wahhabis want, from day one, for you to show them what you are speaking about in spirituality? They will say, "Show it to us." How are you going to see when you are blind? You have to spend fifty, sixty, seventy years in the guidance of a perfect guide, and you have to research—you have to research and believe in what he is showing you in the way of *Sayyīdinā* Muhammad ﷺ; then at one point, that discovery will come, and you will see it like a sun in front of you.

Saints are not like the Prophet ﷺ, but they are inheritors of the Companions and inheritors of the Prophet ﷺ, as *Sayyīdinā* Muhammad ﷺ said in the *hadith*, "Scholars, or saints, are the inheritors of prophets."[34]

What they inherit is the science of guiding, and the knowledge of how to guide their followers to the Presence of *Sayyīdinā* Muhammad ﷺ.

God said:

---

[34] Abū Dāwūd.

O ye who believe! Fear Allah and be with those who are true (in word and deed).[35]

This means to be with the friends of God; the saints. Then you will see miracles. Why? Because God says, in another section of Qur'an:

And for those who fear Allah, He (ever) prepares a way out,
And He provides for him from (sources) he never could imagine.[36]

Allah will give that servant an exit, an opening to the right way. He will reward him and send him sustenance. He will send him sustenance from everywhere, places that he never expected. This sustenance is not only food! It is also spiritual sustenance.

And that's why you must keep the daily personal liturgy and keep your piety. Then doors will open. As these doors open, God sends. That is the meaning of the verse's mention of a "way out." A way out to the next door.

So by doing the personal liturgy every day, one door opens, a second door opens, veils of darkness go away, and God sends you heavenly sustenance. He sends you a special aura. The metaphor is that it pressurizes the "liquid" perfume of all the cells of your body together. When there is a release (like a person pressing the button on a bottle of perfume) then that sweet-smelling gas escapes from your heart, like a mist of perfume, giving a nice smell to everyone.

All of this is because of the daily personal liturgy that the shaykh prescribed to you, beside your obligations, beside your *sunnah* obligations; in addition to everything else that you are doing. He prescribed it specifically to you because everyone has a different treatment that can affect and open these doors.

---

[35] Sūratu 't-Tawbah (Repentance), 9:119.
[36] Sūratu 't-Talāq (Divorce), 65:2-3.

Keeping this daily personal liturgy is the second level, as we have described.

Now if a follower leaves his daily personal liturgy for one day, he has to repent and ask forgiveness. He has left his medication. Similarly, someone with heart disease or cancer must not leave the medication—he has to take it or he will die.

Penalty for Leaving the Daily Personal Liturgy

If the follower forgets, failing to do the daily personal liturgy for one day, he has to perform an *istighfār* for every particle of *dhikr* he missed, whatever the shaykh has prescribed to him for his ability to purify himself through *nawāfil* on the number of those recitations that he is doing, even on each letter of the *juz'* of Qur'an, he has to ask forgiveness, and this is multiplied by 40—he has to do the *istighfār* for forty days if he missed his daily personal liturgy on one day.

The penalty for missing the daily personal liturgy for one day is either (1) based on the number of hours your daily personal liturgy takes per day, or (2) on the number of repetitions in total that you make every day, you must say *astaghfirullāh* for each one. That is, if you say every day 5,000 times "Allah", 1,000 times "*Lā ilāha illa-Llāh*" (hypothetically speaking), 2,000 Ṣalawāt, one *juz'* of Qur'an, one *juz'* of *Dalā'ilu 'l-Khayrāt*, then first you have to ask repentance from God because you left your daily personal liturgy, on the number of every *dhikr* that you missed. You add them all. However many parts of Qur'an you missed, say *astaghfirullāh* for each letter. On *Dalā'ilu 'l-Khayrāt*, you have to say *astaghfirullāh*. And these *istighfār* must be repeated for forty days.

You accumulate the total of every single repetition of every type, including as a separate repetition each letter of the Holy Qur'an that you have as part of your daily personal liturgy—together this may all come to 20,000 *istighfār*. To be excused from that single day that you missed your daily personal liturgy, you have to do perhaps 20,000 *istighfār* for 40 days.

In the army there are special forces soldiers. They are trained differently from everyone else. They are "special forces," real men, very strong—they eat snakes, they eat everything - they will even eat you!

Do you want to reach the level of manhood in *ṭarīqah*? A man or woman who wants to reach the level of manhood (*rujulīyyah*) must keep his or her daily personal liturgy, which is their prescription from the shaykh. Do you want to be a child? Okay then, never mind, be a child; but then you are with the lovers—your shaykh gives you candy, makes you happy, you go. That's it.

Do you want to be a saint? Do you want to be granted to see, when you ask to see? Then you have to follow that harder way. That is the *ṭarīqah* of manhood.

We explained, earlier, the importance of making the daily personal liturgy at one of the three different prescribed times: one hour before the pre-dawn prayer until the sunrise prayer; the late afternoon prayer until the sunset prayer; the sunset prayer to the night prayer. Then he is fulfilling his obligation but he is not being raised to a high level. But he is still in *ṭarīqah*.

How to Make Up for a Day of Missed Daily Personal Liturgy

And as he is performing his daily personal liturgy, God will be dressing him every day with an aura that purifies him and opens veils. We discussed that, veil after veil, veil after veil, day after day, until he will be able to build up his strength in order to get the Light of God in his heart—the light that God sends to the heart of the believer.

God said in Holy Qur'an:

But those will prosper who purify themselves.[37]

Purifying himself means to raise himself, to control his ego and to leave bad manners; then he will be successful—God is assuring people that that person will be successful.

It means: "Verily the one who leaves bad manners is going to reach the highest level of purification of the self." So the importance of leaving bad manners is to put you on the right step, on the second level of the disciplined steps of *ṭarīqah,* in order that saints raise you to the third level, where you can successfully enter the circle of *dhikr*.

So when the shaykh looks at your sickness and prescribes supplications for you and a daily personal liturgy, and makes a code for you, then you must keep it exactly; because it is a code, and if you are off—up by one or down by one—then the door does not open. When you perform the daily personal liturgy with consistency, you have achieved the second level.

[37] Sūratu 'l-'Alā (the Most High), 87:14.

The Third Level—Sincerity, Witnessing, God's Holy Name, Purification

Then there is the third step which is purification, a process of remembering Allah ﷻ. When you are cleaning yourself at the second level, you can then step onto the third level; when veil after veil has been opened—you are now coming to the Station of Sincerity, the Station of Witnessing—where you can see.

So the third level of the ladder (from the nine different steps), is purification of the ego. Through the daily personal liturgy that you are doing, the way of seekers opens for you—now you are inside that circle. And now we will see what is going to open for you.

You are doing your prescribed daily personal liturgy according to the shaykh's orders—taking your "medication," and you begin to feel purity. And when the purity comes, you will find yourself inside the Station of Sincerity—"to worship God as if you are seeing Him."[38]

Now at that level of purification of the self—God is telling you in Holy Qur'an,

But those will prosper who purify themselves.[39]

This verse refers to the person who raised himself up and reaches the third step on that ladder, becoming successful in

---

[38] Bukhari.

[39] Sūratu 'l-'Alā (the Most High), 87:14.

seeing what people cannot see. That is the level at which you have the power of witnessing. There, as soon as he is in that circle, involuntarily—without his forcing himself to remember God's Name, the Name of God comes directly through his whole spirit and body and he will remember; he will call upon his Lord:

And glorify the Name of their Guardian-Lord, and pray.[40]

There he will call upon and mention his Lord – in what name? God says that he mentions the Name of his Lord, but does not mention which Name he uses. What Name? You do not know! For every person it is a different Name. It is not the same Name. It is according to the holy blessing that you have been granted, according to your heart, what kind of a Name God will give you. At that time you reach the real code where you can open and see.

At the beginning you have the code, you enter the code with the daily personal liturgy. Then once you are inside you have another code your shaykhs will give you. They will give you a Name that you can use. When you use that Name, what will happen?

And at that level when the seeker mentions God's Name, he then falls under the meaning of the verse which says to praise the Prophet ﷺ. What kind of prayer is he praying there?

Allah and His angels send blessings on the Prophet: O ye who believe! Send blessings on him, and salute him with all respect.[41]

The seeker now realizes the importance of the Prophet ﷺ because of the reference at the end of the verse to Prophet ﷺ.

And glorify the Name of their Guardian-Lord, and pray.[42]

---

[40] Sūratu 'l-'Alā (the Most High), 87:15.
[41] Sūratu 'l-Aḥzāb (the Confederates), 33:56.

"And pray" is a reference to making prayers on Prophet ﷺ. At that level the saints have brought him to realize that he has to say *Lā ilāha illa-Llāh* – what comes after that? *"Muḥammadun rasūlullāh*—Muhammad is the Messenger of God." Muhammad ﷺ is the door. As soon as you mention God's Name, "and pray"—meaning you pray on Prophet ﷺ—you know that he is your door, he is God's door, he is God's way to Himself. That is why at this point, we understand that the door of God, that you can go through, is *Sayyīdinā* Muhammad ﷺ. That is at that level; later there is another higher level.

"And pray" means he will pray to God—the Prophet ﷺ takes him from the level of the Reality of Prophet ﷺ to the Station of Recognition of Oneness.[43] So the Prophet ﷺ will raise him to the Station of Witnessing, and there he will be able to pray and will be able to see the signs of God everywhere, wherever he turns his face.

So when you are able to understand the Reality of Prophet ﷺ, it means the shaykh is guiding you through the daily personal liturgy that he ordered you to do at the second level, and now he is raising you up to the third level where you are able to purify yourself, going into remembrance of God's Name through the door of Muhammad ﷺ, and that's why the previous verse is:

But those will prosper who purify themselves.[44]

The one who cleans himself and raises himself to the state of purification is successful.

The following verse is:

And glorify the Name of their Guardian-Lord...[45]

---

[42] Sūratu 'l-'Alā (the Most High), 87:15.
[43] Arabic: *maqām at-tawḥīd:* term in Sufism for the station of witnessing the God's Unique Oneness.
[44] Sūratu 'l-'Alā (the Most High), 87:14.

And this verse means that the follower will be able to remember that Name at that level.

Before that, the seeker is remembering Satan's name in *dunyā*—he cannot remember God's Name. If he cannot purify himself, taking the prescription from the shaykh, then his whole intention is still this world. Therefore he cannot yet remember God's Name. First he must escape that sickness using the daily personal liturgy, then the remembrance of God's Name will be opened to him—where he can mention the Name of his Lord.

As soon as he mentions the Name of his Lord, the door of the Prophet ﷺ will become manifest—he will understand that it is needed for him—the door is through *Sayyīdinā* Muhammad ﷺ. There he says,

And glorify the Name of their Guardian-Lord...[46]

As soon as he remembers God's Name in Reality, immediately following the words in Qur'an are "and prays." Prays on whom? He will understand the reality that Muhammad ﷺ is the way for him. It is very important for him to reach that level, where he will begin to praise Prophet ﷺ.

God said that He and His angels are praising the Prophet ﷺ.[47] The seeker at this stage knows that reality, he begins to praise Prophet ﷺ. As he is praising Prophet ﷺ, he will be raised higher.

At that moment he will understand what God said in Holy Qur'an:

Nay (behold), ye prefer the life of this world;[48]

---

[45] Sūratu 'l-ʿAlā (the Most High), 87:15.
[46] Sūratu 'l-ʿAlā (the Most High), 87:15.
[47] Sūratu 'l-Aḥzāb (the Confederates), 33:56.
[48] Sūratu 'l-ʿAlā (the Most High), 87:16.

Allah is saying: "But in reality you see what I am giving you." You see that when you followed a guided shaykh, following the daily personal liturgy essential to the second level, you stepped onto the second step of the ladder. Now you begin to reach the third level, where, by mentioning His Name through purification of the self, you begin to understand the Reality of the Prophet ﷺ, which is the door for the Reality of Oneness.[49]

How much happiness before that did you find in chasing this world!

Nay (behold), ye prefer the life of this world;[50]

It means, "You did not realize that this *dunyā* that you were in was worthless compared to what I am giving you now?" Now at this time, the follower will understand, "Oh, what have I done in the past?" He will begin to bite his fingers. "I regret what I have done in the past, running after worldly things."

You begin to disdain the worldly life, and love the hereafter instead:

But the Hereafter is better and more enduring.[51]

It means that, at that third level, God, with the *barakah* of Prophet ﷺ and the guidance of the shaykh through your prescribed daily personal liturgy, opens for you a window to the afterlife. And now you begin to enjoy and enter the ecstasy of love of the afterlife, receiving fountains of knowledge—you will be dressing with them, one after another.

And this is in the Books of the earliest (Revelation).[52]

---

[49] Arabic: *Ḥaqīqat at-Tawḥīd*: the reality of Divine Oneness.
[50] Sūratu 'l-ʿAlā (the Most High), 87:16.
[51] Sūratu 'l-ʿAlā (the Most High), 87:17.
[52] Sūratu 'l-ʿAlā (the Most High), 87:18.

This was already written—you are going to see it. It means: "What We have given before to Ibrāhīm ﷺ and Mūsā ﷺ and after....it is a fact that you will be able to reach the knowledge of what is before and knowledge of what is after." That is why the Prophet ﷺ said that God "gave me the knowledge of what is before and what is after";[53] and you will begin to be to inherit a small amount of that knowledge, little-by-little according to the capacity your heart. On the third stage of discipline, you reach the understanding that there is no way except through purification of the self.

So you cannot leave one part of the prescribed daily personal liturgy, because then you will fall from the third level, from that high knowledge that God has given you. You will fall and then there is no way for you to repent except by going through more hardship!

And that is why saints prescribe forty days of asking forgiveness for one day of losing your daily personal liturgy, to avoid your losing access to that circle of saints, and that ecstasy of heavenly knowledge. That heavenly knowledge cannot coexist with any crack in your system, any "hole in your pipes," or else all of your knowledge will be thrown away in the garbage, without value and without importance to the follower. For this reason saints always want the follower in the best condition. That is why the follower has to make up for a mistake in his daily personal liturgy over a period of forty days.

So now you are beginning to be able to build up, in the third level, through the Station of Witnessing, what saints open to you. Through purification, you begin to mention God's Name, *"and pray,"* meaning here praising His Prophet ﷺ, because you then

---

[53] Arabic: *ʿulūmu 'l-awwalīna wa 'l-ākhirīn*: knowledge of the "Firsts" and the "Lasts," refers to the knowledge that God poured into the heart of Muhammad ﷺ during his ascension to the Divine Presence.

realize that the door to God is through *Sayyīdinā* Muhammad ﷺ. It is the Prophet ﷺ who brings you to the Reality of Divine Oneness. The Prophet ﷺ is the best and highest one in understanding the reality of God's Divine Oneness. He is the only one who is truly understanding that Oneness, because he went on the Night Journey and Ascension.

If this world is still holding you, you cannot ascend. The Prophet ﷺ went into ascension, until he reached the position described in the verse:

And he was at a distance of but two bow-lengths or (even) nearer;[54]

At that third level, your physical body becomes lighter. Why? Not because you lose weight. No. But, when you begin to be blessed every day, and you are dressed with the garments of the daily personal liturgy, the container of your body becomes stronger – more and more solid, without any more cracks, so, as God is sending His Light to your heart, that Light is becoming stronger and ever stronger. If you have a soda can or a pressurized perfume bottle, when you open it even a little bit the nice scent goes everywhere. It comes out in the form of a gas, because it was under a lot of pressure. It is liquid, but the pressurization makes it come out as a gas, which spreads that smell and its light quickly. Like a laser, it goes everywhere.

So when your body becomes light gravity can no longer affect you. Like a balloon—if you fill it by mouth with air, it will not fly. But if you put helium in it, it will fly. That light that God gives to you in the third level, the Station of Witnessing, after purification of the self—that very strong light will carry your body and take it like a helium balloon. From that light that is lifting you up, it becomes as if you had no weight.

---

[54] Sūratu 'n-Najm (the Star), 53:9.

The Fourth Level—The Station of Gnosis

When you become like a balloon, rising up in the horizon of where the sun of knowledge is rising up—you will be a balloon rising up through your heavenly levels, diffusing, throwing all your garbage character away, and only your purity will be ascending. And you will be dropping all the extra weight that you do not need—the bad characteristics that we explained in other series. When you get rid of them, you become progressively lighter, moving higher in God's horizons, rising like a sun of knowledge, reaching the Station of Gnosis. This gnosis is the opposite of heedlessness.

Gnosis means to know everything—heedlessness means to know nothing.

At this Station of Gnosis, you will be receiving heavenly knowledge in every moment:

> *So they found one of Our servants, on whom We had bestowed Mercy from Ourselves and whom We had taught knowledge from Our own Presence.* [55]

This verse refers directly to *Sayyīdinā* al-Khiḍr and the gnosis he possessed. Similarly, Āṣif ibn Barkhīyya, is mentioned with *Sayyīdinā* Sulaymān in the Qur'an:

> *Said one who had knowledge of the Book: "I will bring it to thee within the twinkling of an eye!"* [56]

---

[55] Sūratu 'l-Kahf (the Cave), 18:65.
[56] Sūratu 'n-Naml (the Ant), 27:40.

The one possessing knowledge of the Book said he could bring the throne of Sheba to *Sayyīdinā* Sulaymān ﷺ (Solomon) in one second. You begin to receive this kind of knowledge.

Therefore, gnosis is the opposite of heedlessness. Heedlessness is ignorance. When you reach gnosis, God does not like you to go back, even for one second, into heedlessness or ignorance—you have to keep moving forward. On that road there will be a lot of temptations, a lot of tests, to see whether you really have achieved the Station of Gnosis. For example, when *Sayyīdinā* Mūsā ﷺ wanted to know more about gnosis, he asked God, and God sent him to *Sayyīdinā* al-Khiḍr ﷺ .

So what did Khiḍr ﷺ do? When they boarded a boat, he made a hole in the boat. So he tested him to see what he would do. And *Sayyīdinā* Mūsā ﷺ said, "Oh! What are you doing?" objecting to Khiḍr's ﷺ actions.

(The other) said: "Verily you will not be able to have patience with me!"[57]

Gnosis will be completely different than normal life. There will be a lot of tests in that station. God will be ordering the Prophet ﷺ, and the Prophet ﷺ will be ordering your shaykh, to find tests for you during your seeking on the way.

Differentiate between Mistakes and Violations

If you make a mistake out of ignorance, people will give you an excuse. But if you know that you cannot park your car in the middle of the road and yet you still park there, they are going to punish you. That is not allowed—it is a gross violation. If you park on the side of the road, the police might give you a ticket, saying, "Oh, he does not know." But if you leave your car in the middle of the road, they will take it away completely! That is not

---

[57] Sūratu 'l-Kahf (the Cave), 18:67.

cause for a ticket anymore, they will confiscate the whole car! So at the Station of Gnosis, when you know—and they are opening for you this knowledge—how can you make mistakes? If you do, you will be punished.

Look at *Sayyīdinā* Ādam. Satan came and tricked him, saying, "Eat from that tree. You have all of Paradise, this tree will make you absolutely ever-living, ever-lasting—eat from it!" Before this happened, *Sayyīdinā* Ādam had knowledge.

God had ordered all the angels to make prostration to him and they did.[58] And despite possessing that gnosis, he still ate from the tree. For that reason, the punishment became greater. "Go to Earth! Don't stay in Paradise anymore."

So this means that if you do something wrong at the Station of Gnosis, they will take it all from you. You will go back to the first level: the Station of Follower. That person has to go all the way back to the first level we described—the first step, not the third nor the second. No!

You have to make a new initiation with the shaykh now. Whatever you have achieved is lost! Your teachers take it completely from your heart—you become heedless. Now another time, go back.

Keep Your Oath with Your Shaykh

And that's why you see that many followers run away. They go, because the shaykh takes everything: "You did not keep your promise with me. My promise—you come back and renew your initiation—if you made the mistake without bad intention – because they put you in the Station of Gnosis, and Satan tricked you and you followed him." Then it is as if you had parked your car in the middle of the road.

---

[58] This was a prostration to show respect, not worship.

But if you did not let Satan approach and you are always seeking God's forgiveness "*Astaghfirullāh, astaghfirullāh*" when you make a mistake—then it is as if you have parked your car by the cross-walk or by the side of the road. But if you accepted the promise of Satan, he tricked you and you followed him, it is as if you put your car in the middle of the road.

But if you did not follow Satan, but made a mistake unintentionally, it is as if you parked your car on the side of the road—you tried your best, but failed. The saints give you a ticket. And what is that ticket? For forty days, it is forbidden, *ḥarām*, for you to eat anything and drink anything except three dates and three cups of water—this is to punish your ego and to tell yourself, "You cannot disobey the discipline of this *ṭarīqah*," so that you can reach these high levels.

For forty days, your daily allowance is to eat three dates and to drink three cups of water! You have to remember how much hardship Prophet ﷺ went through—for many days he and his family never ate. They were wrapping stones on their stomachs in order not to feel the hunger. And if they were successful and found something to eat, they did not eat more than three dates a day. So you have to give your ego a lesson. Follow the Prophet ﷺ. Tell yourself, "Ah, my ego! You are making problems for me? I am going to teach you a lesson. Three dates a day, for forty days, and three cups of water." This is to learn from your role model, the Prophet ﷺ, how terrible was the hardship that Prophet ﷺ and Companions endured in their lives.

If you want to reach the Station of Manhood[59]—that is the level of the elite. Not the elite of worldly, rich people. No. It means rich in knowledge, rich in the afterlife, rich in the love of God; for this you have to discipline yourself. So if you want that

---

[59] Arabic: *Maqāmu 'r-Rijāl*-the station of manhood, in the spiritual sense, power over the self. The term can apply to both males and females.

level, you follow. If you want to stay at the beginner's level—lovers who love the shaykh and come to his meetings—that is something else.

This is Station of Gnosis—the fourth step on the ladder of nine steps of discipline of the Naqshbandi Order. And as we have explained before, that Station of Gnosis is to become a Knower, a Gnostic in Allah's way—knowing about your Lord.

To summarize, the steps to reach the fourth level are:

1. give initiation to the shaykh
2. go through the daily personal liturgy
3. do the daily personal liturgy which will consist of the prescribed spiritual medicine for your bad qualities that the shaykh will prescribe for you.
4. then you reach the Station of Gnosis, where you will know about your Lord.

But before knowing about your Lord—to reach that level, you have to know about yourself. As the Prophet ﷺ said, "Whoever knows himself knows his Lord."[60]

When you are in the way of the Station of Gnosis, your shaykh is guiding you through a tunnel which is filled with veils, opening veil after veil, until you begin to find and describe the mistakes of your ego. You begin to find the difficulties that you are facing coming from your desires and from your ego. You begin a struggle between yourself and your ego. That is what we call the Greater Struggle that the Prophet ﷺ described to his Companions.

---

[60] Related by Shaykh Muḥīyddīn ibn 'Arabī, who said while not authentic from the way of narration it is considered authentic from the way of unveiling (kashf).

His Companions had given their lives for God and His Prophet ﷺ when the Quraysh of Mecca tried to destroy them by declaring war against them. The Companions accompanied the Prophet ﷺ going forth to great battles to defend themselves, their wives and children from those who declared war on them. And in these battles, many died. With all their suffering and all they faced in that military struggle, at the end when returned finally to Madina, the Prophet ﷺ told them:

"Now you have left the smaller Jihad to come to the greater Jihad, *al-Jihād al-akbar*."

The Companions said, "is there a greater Jihad than what we were just in?"

The Prophet replied, "Yes, the Jihad against your self."[61]

Fighting an enemy is easy. They say to you, "This is your enemy. Fight!" You go and fight. Your ego will not struggle against you. You know your enemy, you go and fight him. But to fight your self, to consider your self to be the enemy and to come against it and against your desires, that is harder. Every one of us thinks himself clean, perfect and high. He does not know that his self is his enemy.

Look at what happened to *Sayyīdinā* Ādam ؑ. Satan came, and the ego immediately accepted, agreed, and ate from the tree. Then God sent Ādam ؑ from Paradise to Earth. Your self is your biggest enemy, and it will bring you down to the seven hells.

Success begins when the follower begins to fight his desires, and begins to be able to ride his ego; when he agrees that he is the worst in manners and character, and believes that these worst qualities are embodied in his ego. The ego never accepts to be

---

[61] Ghazālī, in the *Iḥyā'*, al-'Irāqī said that Bayhaqī related it on the authority of Jābir and said: There is weakness in its chain of transmission. According to Nisā'ī in *al-Kunā* is a saying by Ibrāhīm ibn Ablah.

low, never accepts to be humiliated. If someone comes and shouts at you, what do you do? You get angry and fight back, because the ego does not like that. But if someone comes and fights with you and shouts at you and you say nothing, at that time you are controlling your anger, controlling your ego. At that time, God raises you to the level of Gnosis.

If you ask anyone present here, "What do you think about yourself—are you good or bad?" What will they say? "Good!" Of course! If someone comes for prayer and puts the carpet in one direction another comes and says, "No, it is not like this, it should be like that." Then another says, "No, the direction of prayer is a little bit to this way." Another says, "No, the direction of prayer is a little bit the other way." Everyone disagrees with the other. That is a sickness.

To be a knower or a gnostic in the Way of God, you cannot make mistakes. You try your best not to make mistakes. Therefore you must learn all the weaknesses of your self. As the Prophet ﷺ "Whoever knows himself knows his Lord." Whoever knows the mistakes of his ego and controls himself, then God begins to open for him the light of gnosis.

The opposite of the Station of Gnosis is heedlessness. Heedlessness is when you are in the habit of doing everything well, but suddenly without thinking, you lose concentration for a moment and everything goes upside down.

An example of this is when sometimes you see people whose eyes glaze over and fail to focus—this happens to them involuntarily, and they do not know what they are doing. They may be staring into space. Their concentration is gone—that is a big danger. If you are the pilot of an airplane or a boat, and you become a little bit heedless, your whole ship will be upside down in the ocean, or your plane will flip out of the sky.

For *Sayyīdinā* Ādam in just one second, Iblīs, the devil, came and told him to eat from the tree. Heedlessness overcame him, and *Sayyīdinā* Ādam was taken out from Paradise because he disobeyed God. Satan had put him into heedlessness.

THE FIFTH LEVEL—BREAKING ANGER AND OBLITERATING THE EGO

When you reach the level of gnosticism, of knowledge about Allah and His existence, and knowledge of your dependence on Allah ﷻ, then there at that level you have to learn how to control your self—you have to be able to control anger and completely demolish the self—after which the self will never again exist.

We are entering a discussion of the fifth level now; a level where there cannot be any appearance of the self. The self has to be completely demolished. And demolishing the self means that there is no more "me." There is only Allah.

One time, one person called one of the big saints of the Naqshbandi Order, *Sayyīdinā* Abū Yazīd al-Bistāmī ق. He said, "*Yā* Abā Yazīd." Abā Yazīd didn't answer. He was calling him, "Abā Yazīd!" and still Abū Yazīd did not answer. He thought to himself, "Maybe he doesn't want to answer." So he left. The next day he came. He saw him there, and wanting to ask a question called, "O Abā Yazīd!" He didn't answer. "Abā Yazīd!" No answer. "O Abā Yazīd!" He didn't answer. Then he came close. "O Abā Yazīd!" No answer. Touching and moving him, he said, "Abā Yazīd!" Abā Yazīd still didn't answer. Shaking him now, he said, "*Yā* Abā Yazīd!" No answer.

That one was clever. He realized there is something going on. So he said, "*Yā* Abdullah!"

Sayyīdinā Abū Yazīd ق said, "Yes. For forty years I am trying to lose and forget about Abā Yazīd, and two days ago I lost it. Now you want to remind me about Abā Yazīd! After forty years of difficulties, through different levels, I was able to demolish my self completely, and to disappear completely from my name, and now you are bringing me that memory!?

For forty years, Abū Yazīd was trying to get rid of his self. Abū Yazīd al-Bistāmī died during that struggle. Finished. There is no more Abū Yazīd ق, and although the man saw Abū Yazīd in front of him and was shaking him, he was dead.

Nowadays, however, if someone fails to introduce a person with all of the proper titles in front of his name, he will be upset! Next to his name he must see "doctor", "engineer", "PhD", "president", "minister", "prime minister", "officer", or whatever title he has achieved. Everyone must have a title and a name. Some must be "Ḥabīb," some must be "Shaykh." Everything, whether religious or secular, that can be thrown in front of the name must be there.

And even beyond that, if someone is the driver of a president, he wants to put in front of his name, "driver of the president." A speaker today, before he gives a speech, has to give his entire resume beforehand, and the moderator has to mention in introducing him that he studied this and studied that, and attended such-and-such university and is a Ph.D. and is a consultant and a CEO, an FBO, an FMA, or whatever.

Today, I called this man three names: Sukarno, Suharto, Sunatro, Sinarto, Frank Sinatra. He was happy. He didn't say "No, no, no, I am Senarto." No, his attitude was, "Ah, whatever you want to call me, no problem." He is a humble person. Allah likes humble people. He doesn't like arrogant people. Arrogance is bad. It takes you away from the presence of Allah ﷻ.

Iblīs failed his test because he was arrogant. Allah cursed him and threw him away. *Sayyidinā* Ādam ؑ was humble. Allah forgave him and brought him back. Make yourself humble in order that you will be able to reach Allah's ﷻ Divine Presence.

On the fifth level, you have to forget completely who you are. There cannot be two there. There has to be one. One time in Lebanon, it was snowing and very, very cold. I was driving to visit Grandshaykh. We arrived at two o'clock in the morning. It was so cold! We were freezing. So we came to Mawlana Shaykh Nazim's ق house before going to Grandshaykh's house.

We knocked on the door. He came—this was 2:00 in the morning—people are sleeping. But we were "trouble-makers" so we were coming very late. We knocked on the door and Mawlana came to open the door. Now the houses there are not like here. There is an outside door—you have to walk through the snow to get to it. He came out and he said, in Arabic, "Who is that?" I said, "Me." As soon as I said "me," I didn't hear anything. He went back. He didn't open the door. So we were waiting....five minutes, ten minutes. He had been right there! He had spoken to us!

So I knocked again. There was no bell. You have to knock on the door. You have to hit the door. He came again, and said, "Who is that?" I said, "Me." He left.

Then, a third time I knocked, he came, and he said, "Who is that?" I understood what he wanted. I said, "You!" He said, "Yes, now I open the door. Because there is no 'me and you' here. There is either me or you. You, no. Because you are a follower. There must be 'me,' here."

He was teaching that in Allah's Presence, the servant has no existence. The existence is only for Allah ﷻ. The servant is a slave for his Lord. So on that fifth level there is no existence of the self. You have to demolish it completely and come to your Lord—"O my Lord—You are the One, the Creator. I am nothing, zero. Not even zero, less than zero."

That is Physics. Zero is only a number to show that something exists. Even zero exists. Be less than zero.

This puts down anger. When you do not exist anymore, you do not see yourself anymore. Then whatever happens in front of you in this world makes no difference, it will not make you angry—that is finished.

You cannot be angry with anything except with your self. Be angry with yourself. But you have no right to be angry with any person on earth. Because on that fifth level the shaykh is sending tests on you by order of the Prophet ﷺ The Prophet ﷺ is sending to the shaykh, and Allah ﷻ is sending to the Prophet ﷺ—to test you, how patient can you be and how much can you refrain from anger. So they will send every kind of test. Even though you are a big saint, they will send you tests, to see if you get upset or not.

The hardest test of anger is not whether you will fight with someone you do not know on the street. That is easy. He shouts at you, but you keep quiet, and move on. However, when your shaykh gets angry with you, and shouts at you, and kicks you out from his presence, and says, "You are not my *murīd* anymore! Don't show me your face! Go from here! You are the worst, sick one here! Go away! I don't want to see you!" When he says all of that, your face must not change. You must be smiling. Your love must not change to the shaykh. Even if he is really scolding you. You must not change. If your face changed, you failed.

One time, when I was young, I was coming and visiting Grandshaykh, Shaykh Abdullah al-Fa'iz ad-Daghestani ق. His mosque is beside his house and there is a small road, perhaps one yard across, or one and a half yards, between the house and the mosque. And to come to his house you have to pass under his window. And he was shouting, shouting, shouting! Oh! Oh! Oh!

"I don't want to see you here! I don't want you to come to my presence! You are not my follower! You are not my *murīd*! You are nothing! Don't show me your face!"

He was shouting at someone. Oh. Me—I could not move anymore. I was stuck, because if you move from such a position... If he is shouting at that one like that, what about if he shouts at you? You cannot move anymore, because any movement, he will hear you. It is under his window. So until he was finished...

I knew he was shouting at Mawlana Shaykh Nazim. Finally the shouting stopped and Mawlana Shaykh came out from Shaykh Abdullah's door. So as Mawlana was coming down, he had to pass by the masjid. So he saw me. He looked at me, and he was laughing. Oh! Despite all this shouting and scolding and Grandshaykh's kicking him out! It was as if nothing had happened. So we went up. As soon as we went up Grandshaykh called saying, "Let them come. Let them come in." So we came, and he was laughing.

Falsehood and Truth

It is impossible for falsehood to be with truth. Always the truth is high, and never can anything go above it. There is a saying: "truth is above all and nothing goes above truth."

Allah also said:

And say: "truth has (now) arrived, and falsehood perished: for falsehood is (by its nature) bound to perish."[62]

So falsehood has to go down. The self is always pushing you to get desires. Satan is always playing with the ego. So when you know your self, when you know the bad characteristics of your self, you eliminate its bad characteristics, and then there is no more falsehood in you. There is only the appearance of truth, the appearance of Allah's justice and knowledge in you. When that happens, you are on the way of gnosticism. When you are in the way of gnosticism, you know that nothing is existing other than

---

[62] Sūratu 'l-Isrā (the Night Journey), 17:81.

Allah ﷻ—so how are you going to get angry or upset with someone when you know that everything was planned by Him?

Allah planned the good, and the evil came because we left the good. So how are we going to come against each other with anger, when we know everything comes from Allah? One of the elements of faith is to believe in destiny, the good and the bad.[63] Everything is planned. If Allah planned that you will be good, He will give you goodness through your life. If you follow Satan, badness will come to you in this world, and that is why anger comes inside us like fire, burning us.

You cannot leave anger without demolishing the bad desires of the ego, because the ego always takes you to follow bad desires, which in turn lead you to anger. So without demolishing the whole structure of your ego, your anger will still live inside the building that you have made of egoism or selfishness, because anger comes from what? When I think "I am right," I think "I am the best." I think "I am the perfect one." I think "I am proud of myself." When I am arrogant I cannot accept anyone pointing out any weakness I may have or shaming me at all. Why do I get upset? Because I think that I am the hugest one.

Your ego/self teaches you hidden association—it says, "Don't accept anyone except yourself. Say, 'There is no god but me.' 'There is nothing other than me.'

Prophet ﷺ came to say to everyone, there is no god but God. "There is no one except God." It means there is no existence except Allah. You cannot say that you have existence. Then you are making association—your self with Allah ﷻ.

---

[63] See the "Gabriel hadith," Bukhari, stating that faith (*īmān*) is to believe in Allah, His angels, His prophets, Holy Books, the Day of Judgment, and destiny, the good and the evil of it.

Why do people fight and have wars? Because everyone says, "There is no one except me. I know everything. Everyone else is wrong, I am right. Everyone else is weak, I am strong. Everyone else is nothing, I am the one who is everything." That creates complete madness in the world, anger—and this anger goes back and forth between those who fight as they fight each other.

Sufi people are peaceful. They know Allah planned everything. Allah said in Qur'an:

> *And (the unbelievers) plotted and planned, and Allah too planned, and the best of planners is Allah.*[64]

They plan, and Allah plans, and Allah is the Best of Planners. So what are you going to plan? What Allah has planned is going to work. What you plan, do not think that it will work? It is not going to work. What Allah has written for you, before He created you, that is what will work. Or else, zero.

Today, technology gives you the example. When you have a computer, you get it clean from the company that sells it—they put software in it. With these programs, the computer functions properly. You will never be able to do anything by yourself without that software. It is impossible. Is that correct? So if you try to put something different from yourself—you invent something, thinking you are a genius—what will happen? All the software will crash, and the whole computer will crash. Now you have to reinstall the software that was there. You cannot add by yourself to what the engineers and computer scientists planned. They know better than you.

So what do you think about Allah ﷻ?

When you understand that everything has been planned, then why will you get upset? For what? If you get upset or do not get

---

[64] Sūrat Āli-ʿImrān (the Family of ʿImrān), 3:54, See also, 27:50 "*They plotted and planned, but We too planned, even while they perceived it not.*"

upset, what is written is going to happen. Look at the flood that came here (to Indonesia). A little bit of a flood. Can you stop it? Even if the whole country comes to stop the flood, they cannot stop it.

Slowly it was rising up.....two feet, three feet, then four feet. Can you stop it? What Allah planned, He planned—you cannot stop it. You went to your home, you came, and the water level was four feet. The next day you came, and the water was up to the ceiling. Can you do anything?

Don't think that Allah planned anything without wisdom. You think that those poor people who were flooded out of their homes will not be rewarded in this life and hereafter? It was the poorest people who had the flood! The rich didn't care. Nothing happened to them. They are living in their palaces. Only the poor—why? Because Allah ﷻ loves poor people.

Allah ﷻ made these poor people the scapegoats for the entire country. And because they carried that burden, Allah saved the rest. They are going to be the first in Paradise on Judgment Day.

Now people are going to the ruined homes of the poor, and giving them a little bit of rice. As if they are helping them, although they have in their homes millions of dollars; really they go there to show off. They give a little bit of rice. On Judgment Day, these poor people will show the rich people the mercy of Allah ﷻ by helping the rich ones to enter Paradise by virtue of that small bit of rice that they gave.

Thankful Rich

Allah loves the 'thankful rich'. Many Muslims who are rich are thankful to Allah, and they are always helping people. Allah ﷻ is merciful. He loves these people also. It is not only the poor, but Allah loves those who help. So anyone helping, Allah ﷻ will save him on Judgment Day. For these poor people, that flood cleaned their sins. Allah might clean all their sins with that flood.

Not only them, but also their ancestors, and send them to Paradise. Can you change what Allah wrote?

So whatever is written in your 'computer', you are going to see. So why do you get upset? Saints understand that reality. And now scientists understand it through their study of DNA. The DNA is like a chip which has your blueprints. All your blueprints for your actions in this world are written there—DNA is like the blueprint of a building, containing your entire life. Everything is written there.

Scientists say that one piece of DNA can contain more than 1 million books.

Recognizing that everything is written, you will try to keep your anger down. Anger was described by Prophet ﷺ as unbelief. Anger makes you an unbeliever because it takes away from you your common sense. With it you lose your common sense—it can even make you kill.

In *ṭarīqah,* you cannot be angry with anyone. If you are angry, you will go back to earlier levels. Even though you may have reached the fifth level, you have to go back to the first level.

The Story of the Wrestler and the Apple Tree

One strong Muslim came to Grand Grandshaykh in Daghestan. He was a wrestler. He said, "I want *ṭarīqah.*" And Grandshaykh said, "We don't give *ṭarīqah* to people like you. You are a wrestler." He had a sword here, a big knife here, and his turban was cocked at an angle. He said, "Shaykh, I want *ṭarīqah.* Give me *ṭarīqah!*" Grandshaykh Sharafuddin said, "There is no *ṭarīqah,* I cannot give you *ṭarīqah.*"

The wrestler put his hand on his sword. His intention is that the shaykh is going to die now, if he doesn't accept to teach him *ṭarīqah.*

At that moment, it came to that shaykh's heart from the Prophet ﷺ, "That man sincerely wants *ṭarīqah,* give it to him. Show him the way."

He said, "Tonight you rest, tomorrow I will show you". So the shaykh was looking at him that night and all night he didn't sleep; he so was excited to receive *ṭarīqah* the next day.

In the morning Grandshaykh told him, "I am sending you today to learn. For three days I will teach you. And then I will see if you want *ṭarīqah."*

He told him, "Go to the market. Walk all the way down the mountain to the village—you will see someone carrying on his shoulders intestines and the feet of goats and lambs. He is a butcher. Come from behind—your hand is big, since you are a wrestler—and beat him on his neck."

The wrestler was very happy. He was a big wrestler. He said, "*Allahu Akbar*! Oh, this *ṭarīqah* is very good. I am going to beat him completely. Finished."

Then, exactly as the shaykh described—at the exact place and time, he saw that man. He came behind him and beat him on his shoulders and neck as he had been ordered. The man looked, and his face was angry but he didn't say a word, and he continued with his work. That wrestler was disappointed. He was hoping for a fight, then to beat him more!

He went back and explained to the shaykh what happened, and the shaykh said, "Okay, stay here tonight." The next day after the early morning prayer, he said, "Okay, you go to the market, but to a different place. You will find someone carrying the insides of lambs' stomachs—dirty food. When you see him, give him a big hit on the shoulder with all your power."

The wrestler was happy—this was better than the first one. He went, found the man as the shaykh described, and beat him very hard. Everything fell down, broken—all the clothes of the man became dirty and very smelly from the insides of the animal. And that man who was beaten looked at the wrestler and was laughing. *Allahu Akbar!*

The wrestler was angrier than before—this one is laughing! At least the other one was upset. He came to the shaykh, and told him what had happened.

The shaykh said, "Never mind, tomorrow, I'll send you somewhere else."

The next day, he told him, "Okay, today do not go to the market, go to a farm instead. You will see an old man, maybe 90 years old. He is very old. He is plowing his field, driving his ox to plow the dirt. This time, take a stick with you. Beat him. Do not come back to me until that stick breaks!

The wrestler was very happy. He said, "Oh, you are my shaykh now. I am very happy, I am going to break the stick on him. That is nice." He liked such shaykhs.

So he went with the stick the next day, and where the shaykh told him to look he found the old man, plowing. He came from behind, and hit him very hard. As he beat him, the old man did not look back, only he pushed the plow faster, making his ox move faster. He beat him again, and he beat on the ox again. He beat him a third time, and the stick broke. When the stick broke, it hurt the wrestler's hand.

The old man stopped working, came running to him and kissed his hand, saying, "O my brother, forgive me. I made your hand feel pain. I am sorry. My shaykh knows too well what my sins are—he sent you here and Allah made you an instrument to clean me, so I feel that I hurt your hand when you were beating me. Your hand was hurt while cleansing me of my sins. Forgive me. Don't be my enemy on Judgment Day, ask Allah's forgiveness for my hurting your hand!"

That wrestler changed completely. He went to the shaykh crying.

The shaykh said, "O my son, the first one was a beginner in *ṭarīqah.* He looked at you with anger. He knows that the shaykh is testing him, but he is still angry. If he had said one word to you, he would have been dropped from that fifth level back to the first. The second one is at the station of an intermediate student, the level of readiness, *musta'id*; he is ready to climb to the sixth level. He is deep in the fifth level. That's why he was laughing, thinking "Yeah. I know. My shaykh sent you to me." So still he has ego there, because he is proud of his actions, but never mind, he is still on the way. So he is a "ready" one, ready to go from that level to the sixth level.

The third one is fully a *murīd,* a disciple. And not only a *murīd,* but a *murīd* with unveiling. He reached the fifth level, and now he is on the sixth level, entering deep inside. He knew that his shaykh sent you to hit him in order to progress more, to be able to jump from the fifth level to the sixth. Without that test he would not have been able to progress. That test made him jump to the sixth level, and that is why he was running to you, kissing your hand. He understood who was behind that test. He knew that you can never reach honey unless you endure the stings of bees.

So through these difficulties, if you don't overcome them, being patient without showing anger, you cannot eat honey. This is *ṭarīqah.* Do you want to eat honey? You have to be stung by bees then—meaning you have to carry difficulties and face obstacles.

Grandshaykh took him to the garden, showing him an apple tree and said, "Take a stone." He picked up a stone.

Grandshaykh said, "Throw it at the apple tree with all your strength." The wrestler threw the stone at the apple tree. A branch broke and fell down with ten apples on it. He said to him, "This is our *ṭarīqah;* if someone harms you, your reply is by sending fruit to him, rewarding him because he harmed you for your benefit. Allah is going to reward you because if you are patient through the harm, He is going to raise you—because you did not create confusion.

So in our *ṭarīqah,* if someone comes to you and harms you, don't harm him back in revenge. Forget about revenge. Allah said about Prophet ﷺ,

We sent thee not, but as a Mercy for all creatures.[65]

Allah sent Prophet ﷺ as a mercy to all the worlds. You have to be merciful. And Allah said, according to the hadith of Prophet ﷺ,

> The Prophet said, "When Allah created the Creation, He wrote in His Book--and He wrote (that) about Himself, and it is placed with Him on the Throne--'Verily My mercy overcomes My anger.'"[66]

So mercy always comes first, not revenge. So like this apple tree—you break the branch, and still it brings you fruit—you have to be like that. Then you understand what is *ṭarīqah.* Then you can understand what initiation with a shaykh is.

If we want to elaborate more on this level, we can continue talking about it for hours and hours and days and days. It will continue, never finishing.

---

[65] Sūratu 'l-Anbīyā (the Prophets), 21:107.
[66] Bukhari.

THE SIXTH LEVEL—ENERGY, ABLUTION, AND COMMUNICATION BY LIGHT

And now we go to the sixth discipline which is very important in the Naqshbandi *ṭarīqah,* and in your daily life—it is that you always have to be completely ready—completely aware of your enemy. When the enemies want to attack you, you must always be ready to retaliate against them.

In the military, there are different divisions which only the commander-in-chief knows. These divisions are established so that the military is always ready to monitor everything around it, so that it will not make one mistake. Because if you make one mistake in the war, the enemy will take over. So they are very careful. They have some specially trained as snipers. They have some who are Special Forces. They have the Navy; they have the Air Force; they have rockets, missiles and tanks. They have every kind of weapon available. And now they have more—AWACS airplanes, and pilot-less airplanes. So they are advancing and developing new technology in order to be more aware of every movement of the enemy, so that they can attack it.

Not only that. They have also produced an intelligence division whose work is to collect information—nothing else. Then they analyze the intelligence they have in order to use it to protect their own forces and to know what the enemy is thinking ahead of time—to analyze where he wants to go and where he wants to attack.

Allah ﷻ said, *"Satan is to man an avowed enemy."*[67] That is it. Finished. There is no other description of him. Your enemy has been described. And you cannot see the devil. You cannot see him moving, you cannot understand how he is playing games. You don't know his tricks. So because of this, you have to carry all the weaponry that Allah ﷻ has given to you through His message to *Sayyīdinā* Muhammad ﷺ, and through what *Sayyīdinā* Muhammad ﷺ has shown us, and what saints have prescribed to us, in order to protect ourselves against Satan.

When you go to a place with cold weather, you wear very thick coats to protect your body to avoid getting sick.

The sixth level is to teach you the discipline that saints show you for collecting information in order to develop an intelligence-gathering system to protect yourself from the tricks of Satan and to know ahead of time what he is preparing against you.

How do you collect information? You must have a "telecommunications" system. If you don't have one, no information is coming to show you the strategy of his tricks. In order to get information you have to have the right channels pouring into your heart. That sixth level is the level of pouring information, "telecommunication" between the *murīd* and the shaykh, through his or her heart. This system must have all its channels open.

And the system does not work in analog form. It works digitally, so that you can receive in your heart, in one moment, information on thousands of stations of saints, all at the same moment. At the same moment you can see them all digitally, and understand them all, like a satellite dish that can get you thousands of television channels. In the past, such things were impossible. You could get one or two channels. Now you can get

---

[67] Sūratu 'l-Isrā (the Night Journey), 17:53.

thousands of channels at the same time. But still you can only focus on one at a time. But all of them come in at the same time.

A powerful high-technology computer can register all of the incoming signals at the same time, and screen them all at the same time. It can screen all these digital channels, and at any instant pull out whatever information you want—all at the same moment, in parallel. If Allah gave it to people to create such computers, then what do you think about Allah's creation, the heart? Will it not work like that, or better?

When you turn on your computer, it takes some time to come on—it does not come on immediately. It may take one minute to reload its operating system, and then you can begin to get messages and information through it.

That sixth level is the level of energy of *ṭarīqah.* Everything there works on light. There is nothing other than light there. The intelligence system that saints are working with is millions of time more powerful than what worldly scientists are inventing. What God has given them, this use of light, is the use of what God has granted to be under the control of humanity.

As God said in Holy Qur'an:

> *Do ye not see that Allah has subjected to your (use) all things in the heavens and on earth, and has made his bounties flow to you in exceeding measure, (both) seen and unseen?*[68]

God gave this to saints. He also gave to everyone, but you cannot use this power. You are still trying to improve, therefore you are still vulnerable to Satan playing with you. Saints can use that power because Satan has no control on them, or very minimal control.

---

[68] Sūrah Luqmān, 31:20, See also, 45:13.

God is the Light, an-Nur, the Source of energy. Light, as we know in physics, is a form of energy, an aspect of energy which we are able to detect. The source of energy gives you light. For example a spotlight is the source and it gives you the light. So that level for saints is the source of energy; they enter inside that ocean and come out as reflectors of light.

And that is why you are attracted to saints. Why are you attracted to them? Because of the Divine light with which they are dressed. Where is that level? In the Ocean of Power, *qudrah,* from which God created creation. From that Ocean of Power, the power of creation, saints can enter into that place. When they enter it, they become reflectors of that energy.

If you put a steel bar in a fire, heating it, it glows when you take it out. In the same way, when they enter into that source and come out, they glow with light.

When you enter that level, you have to prepare yourself. You cannot enter without preparation in order to be always ready and aware of the information that will come to you from the light the saints are bringing, reflecting light from the source of the Ocean of Power.

You have to prepare yourself so that Satan will not trick you. Can Satan go to that place? Of course, Satan can reach everywhere. God gave Satan that power to test God's followers; to test His servants. Satan even came to Prophet Muhammad ﷺ. And Prophet ﷺ blew on him and threw him away. Satan even came to Ādam ﷷ in Paradise. So yes, Satan comes at anytime. Don't say, "A saint is a saint, he is perfected and does not make sins." No, he can still sin. If Satan tricks him, he will make a sin.

And God thereby shows the saint even, "You are still weak!" Whenever a saint reaches a high level, he still makes sins, being weak and helpless. He knows that God is the greatest, and he knows that God made the Prophet, *Sayyīdinā* Muhammad ﷺ truly great. So saints know they are weak servants; but our duty is that if we see them doing something wrong according to our understanding, then we have to excuse them, because they did not do it with a bad intention.

There is no one free of sin, *masʿūm,* except the prophets. All messengers are innocent of sin, protected against making sins. Anyone else can sin, but repent. Saints immediately know if they commit something wrong, and repent.

Nowadays people say, "Ah, who cares! Do not worry, this world is still running on and on!"

Prepare yourself against Satan. The enemy of mankind is Satan. What is the weapon that you can use against Satan so that at anytime you can finish him? God created Satan from fire. The one thing Satan is afraid of is water. To protect yourself from Satan you have to keep water with you all the time, and the means to do this is keeping ablution, *wuḍū*.[69] Your ablution must be with you for twenty-four hours—never lose it. When you lose your ablution, immediately make another one.

Don't say, "Ah never mind, when prayer time comes I will make ablution." No, Satan is waiting. Satan can enter from any cell of your body because these cells are open and energy and light from the air enters from any part of the body. To cover that and to make Satan afraid, use water.

All the cells of your body are open until water comes, God can seal your body completely, just as today they paint wood with sealants, especially boats, so that water cannot penetrate. Similarly ablution is a sealant on your body that prevents Satan from entering.

---

[69] Arabic: *wuḍū:* Ritual ablution in preparation for worship.

When that ablution is there, Satan cannot come to you. When he sees that you always have ablution, he cannot approach you. He wants to find a time when you are heedless of your ablution, even for one second, then he will jump on you. Without ablution there is no protection, with ablution there is protection. And that is why the Prophet ﷺ recommended that even if you have ablution, when you go to prayer make another ablution— "ablution over ablution is light over light."[70]

So with more ablution you become more light, meaning you have thicker protection against Satan.

> When God praised Prophet Muhammad ﷺ on his Night Journey, he saw a huge group of people that had spots of light on their body shining everywhere and he asked about these people and Jibril ؑ said,
>
> "O Messenger of God, this is your community. In this way God differentiates them from others. These people did not allow their ablution to be lost in *dunyā*."

Some saints took their trusts because of ablution. Satan could not approach them. And they were able to get this information system fully into their hearts, fully on that sixth level. When they entered as followers, and they were aware of what was going on and protecting themselves, they were able to get that information. Their ablution was always there. So the weapon to fight your enemy Satan is to keep ablution. They kept their ablution always for twenty-four hours, even when they want to go to bed, they make ablution and slept. Even there if their ablution was gone because they touched their wife, or whatever, it is written that they slept with ablution and they will wake up as if they were in ablution during their sleep.

---

[70] Al-Ghazālī mentioned it in his *Revival of the Religious Sciences (Iḥyā al-'Ulūm ad-Dīn)*.

Anyone who is on ablution in sleep, Satan cannot approach him, and God will take the soul of that servant under the Throne and he will be in prostration under the Throne until he wakes up. It will be written for him that he was a servant there, always in prostration to his Lord. From the time he sleeps until the time he wakes up, it is written for him that he is in worship. Not like the worship of wakefulness when we say, "*Allahu Akbar*!" and our minds go everywhere. When we sleep with ablution our souls will be in prostration, pure and full worship. Ablution is very important as a weapon for the follower or for the servant in general.

When he loses his ablution, he has no right to speak before taking another ablution. He must make a new ablution and must pray two cycles of prayer for the ablution,[71] or else he will be disrespecting that ablution. It is God's obligation. The priority for God is worship, not worldly matters. So when you lose your ablution, quickly make a new ablution without speaking to anyone. You have to do your ablution, pray the *sunnah* of ablution and then you are allowed to go forward.

And I will quickly mention, God said in Holy Qur'an, "*Take your nice clothing to every mosque that you go.*"[72] God made this world a mosque—everywhere you go is a mosque. The entire earth is a mosque. So whenever you lose your ablution, you have to take that "clothing" or "decoration" back, you have to take your best dress; and the best dress with which to come to God is ablution. How are you going to come to Him with torn clothing? Can you go to an interview with your president, government minister or police without nice clothing? You must put on your best clothing; also, you may put on the national dress to meet the president in order to show respect. Respect for saints, respect for

---

[71] This prayer is called "*Sunnatu 'l-wuḍū.*"

[72] Sūratu ' l-ʿArāf (the Heights), 7:31.

ṭarīqah, respect for Shari'ah, respect for Prophet Muhammad ﷺ, respect to God—in order to show this respect, keep your ablution always.

I have only created jinn and men, that they may serve Me. [73]

Everything we do is worship. Eating and drinking are also worship, because we have to give energy to our bodies to perform formal worship. Talking is worship, because we talk about what is best for the community; how to build it, how to establish its infrastructure. Therefore, ablution is necessary. It is not accepted, even in Shari'ah, let alone in *ṭarīqah,* to drink, eat or talk without ablution. By doing this we protect ourselves from Satan at every moment.

So at the sixth level, the weapon to protect yourself against Satan and to establish your system of intelligence is to keep your weapon of ablution ready. This way you are aware in every moment of his tricks. So you have to keep him out of you, and prevent him from fooling you. To do this, you must keep your ablution for twenty-four hours.

He will try to prevent you, using tricks, from making ablution—to preserve his means of entering your cells quickly. Even in the bathroom of a fancy home or hotel, you will find a telephone—because he wants to get you to speak without ablution. If I am speaking with you from Mecca, and you are in the bathroom of your house with the telephone, "*As-salaam 'alaykum!*" "*Wa 'alaykum salaam,* how are you, 'Alī!"

You are in the bathroom breaking your ablution and talking on the phone to Mecca! And there are even more ways! They make a small portable phone that you can keep with you anywhere you go. Even when you are in the shower! They have a waterproof cell phone. You are talking on the phone, "Hello!"

---

[73] Sūratu 'dh-Dhārīyāt (the Winds that Scatter), 51:56.

and you are naked. "Who is calling?" Maybe the minister of religion has called you and you are speaking to him about religion; yet you are in the shower.

One of our grandshaykhs used to do *dhikr* under water in a well because Satan could not disturb him there. He would make *dhikr*, go up and get a breath, go back down, make *dhikr*, go up and get another breath. Because on that level you must remain completely aware of Satan so that he will not trick you.

Ablution will protect you from this kind of enemy, and from Satan, and let you receive energy information from saints to your heart. So do not ever talk, drink, eat, or walk, drive, or fly without ablution. At all times, keep your perfection with you, and your perfection is ablution.

In other sessions, we have already discussed the nine different disciplines that saints make as conditions for seekers in the way of God, following the footsteps of Prophet Muhammad ﷺ. We have to follow these principles, in addition to all the obligations that Shari'ah has taught us. Prophet Muhammad ﷺ has taught us these practices, which although they are not obligations, we must still observe. We must observe these practices as many others have done before us; especially as the Prophet Muhammad ﷺ was doing them always and he was the one who originally taught these practices. They are not obligations, but we have to follow them to be in the Way of God. We have already explained six of them, the last of which was ablution.

And we said that we have to always keep our ablution twenty-four hours a day and that ablution is the weapon of the believer against Satan, because the only way to prevent Satan reaching us is by keeping our ablution. That was the sixth level that we have explained in detail.

THE SEVENTH LEVEL—STRICT AWARENESS OF *HALAL* AND *HARAM*

Now we come to the seventh level. The way to progress is to go from the first level to the second; then to the third and so on until you reach the last.

The seventh level is to have the obligation to look at what is *ḥalāl* and what is *ḥarām* and to distinguish and choose between them. God has forbidden many things, including adultery, theft, lying, gambling, drinking blood, eating pork and eating animals that died (i.e. were not slaughtered). God has forbidden us to touch such actions.

We have to know what is good for us and what is bad for us. Many people are going to be surprised by what I say. Every person before he prays, makes ablution. Can you pray without ablution? No! Prayer is a form of worship to God. To worship Him you have to be clean. The cleanliness comes through ablution. God ordered us to clean ourselves after using the bathroom, and ordered us to make ablution. Many people go into the bathroom at a market, and then do not clean themselves. Satan is playing with them, saying, "Take this little bit of paper and go. Finished!"

The sixth level is the level of information, where you begin to learn the strategy of Satan so you can avoid it. You have to have complete ablution to avoid him. You cannot touch anything without ablution. Saints, keep (and have kept in the past) their ablution for twenty-four hours.

One of the four imams used to keep his ablution from the time of the pre-dawn prayer (Ṣalātu 'l-Fajr) until after the night prayer (Ṣalātu 'l-'Ishā) He would try not to break his ablution and whenever prayer-time came he would make a new ablution over the previous one. He was afraid of Satan's approach, so he kept his ablution like that. He would just make additional ablutions when it came time for a new prayer.

It is *ḥarām* to pray without ablution and anything related to prayer that you do is not accepted unless you have ablution.

I am coming to the seventh level. But first I have to prepare you by speaking about the power to see and communicate over great distances using spiritual means.

The Prophet's caliph *Sayyīdinā* 'Umar ؓ was able to see his army in Damascus; 1,000 miles away from Medina, he saw one of his generals, Sāriyyah, losing a battle against the aggressor.

> Ibn 'Umar ؓ said that his father, *Sayyīdinā* 'Umar ؓ, was delivering a sermon on Friday. In the middle of his sermon, he shouted, "*Yā Sāriyyah, al-jabal*! O Sāriyyah! [look towards] the mountain!" Then he resumed his sermon …
>
> Some people looked at each other in dismay. *Sayyīdinā* 'Alī ؓ said to them, "He will likely say (something) about this statement."
>
> When the people had finished the prayer, they asked *Sayyīdinā* 'Umar ؓ about the incident. He said, "The idea crossed my mind that the enemy aggressors had defeated our brethren and they would run towards the mountain. Thus, if the Muslims moved towards the mountain, they would have to fight on one side only, while if they advanced, they would be destroyed. So those words escaped my mouth."
>
> After a month, a messenger came with good news. He said, "The people of the army heard *Sayyīdinā* 'Umar's ؓ voice on

that day. We all went towards the mountain and God made us victorious."[74]

Another example was *Sayyīdinā* Sulayman ﷺ when he wanted the throne of Sheba. A jinn said, "I can bring it but it will take twenty-four hours." Then Āṣif ibn Barkhīyyah ق said, "I can bring it in the blink of an eye." The man that has the knowledge of the book of Dāwūd ﷺ was able to bring the throne in one second. If he was able to do this with only the knowledge of the book of Dāwūd ﷺ , what do you think of one who has the knowledge of Qur'an?

One time one of the grandshaykhs of the Naqshbandi *ṭarīqah* was with his followers teaching and he said, "Glorified be God, the Ka'bah is not in its place. It is visiting me and circumambulating around me."

Many followers did not believe this and left him, while others stayed. The shaykh kept quiet. Those who stayed said to those who ran away, "Do not object to the shaykh; if you do not believe, then wait until those who are on Hajj come back and we will ask them whether or not they saw Ka'bah there." They waited until they came back and then asked them about the time and moment that their shaykh had said that.

"Did you see something extraordinary in Mecca?" And they said all people were circling there and for one or two seconds the Ka'bah disappeared. Saints have miraculous power. But people are so involved with *dunyā* that it becomes their only interest. They are interested in how they can make money, how they can become political, how they can be famous, how they can have this or do that. There is no longer anything spiritual left.

---

[74] Narrated in *Life of the Companions*, by Shaykh Zakarīya Kandhalvī, from Imam Aḥmad.

So when they heard this confirmation, those followers came back and apologized to the shaykh. He said, "Never mind." Then he told them, "Take a shower and come to me clean." When they came, not one word came from his mouth. And he said, "Now the Ka'bah is coming to our presence. Ka'bah is coming, turning around us three times, leaving its door and then the Ka'bah is going back to Mecca."

There is another story about two followers of the Naqshbandi Order in the time of Grand Grandshaykh. These two followers never lost their ablution, and they both reached the level of *murīd* in the Naqshbandi Order. Then they increased to the level of shaykh. With that they were able, when they said "*Allahu Akbar*!" to see the Ka'bah in front of them. As they were improving more and more, when they said "*Allahu Akbar*" they found themselves inside the Ka'bah.

So these two followers were able to move to Ka'bah and come back home. They always used to argue with each other, not as enemies but to test each other. One day they were preparing themselves to go to the Ka'bah. One said, "You are able to go to Ka'bah and back because I help you." The other would say, "No, it is because I help you that you are able to go to Ka'bah and back." Back and forth they argued.

Then the time for prayer came and they said "*Bismi'l-Lāhi 'r-Raḥmāni 'r-Raḥīm*" and they prayed, went there and came back. Their wives were listening to this. And both of the wives said, "these two husbands that we have, they did not reach to that level except because of us. If we were not the ones that helped them to go there, they never would have been able to reach the Ka'bah or to go inside."

The women also were Naqshbandi followers of that Shaykh, so they knew. Now the women planned a trick for their husbands to show them that it was actually their work that made this possible. Usually these two men would eat before going to pray at the Kaʿbah.

So this time the two women cooked and gave food to their husbands; but they did not take showers, or have ablution. Then the time for Friday prayers came, and *"Allahu Akbar"* they had to go. One says, *"Bismi'l-Lāhi 'r-Raḥmāni 'r-Raḥīm, Allahu Akbar*!" but he found himself on the highway; and the other was not able to go anywhere. What happened? Every time before they had been able to go. They began to think about what had happened today that was different from yesterday.

Their wives said, "We have served you for many years and God made everything easy for you and God gave you all this. We never gave you food without taking a complete shower and complete ablution. We kept our ablution and shower especially when we were cooking. Because of that God gave you that power. You were thinking that you achieved your high levels by yourselves, but we wanted to show you that without our help you would not have been able to achieve what you have achieved. So today, we did not take showers before cooking. We did not make ablution or say *"Bismi'l-Lāhi 'r-Raḥmāni 'r-Raḥīm"* while cooking; and we did not make praise on the Prophet ﷺ *ṣalawāt,* while cooking.

That is why they were unable to move. This means that at the seventh level of discipline in the Naqshbandi Order, you cannot eat food cooked by someone without ablution. You cannot eat food from someone who has taken no shower. You cannot eat food from someone who is not praising God. You cannot eat food from the street, where you do not know if they are smoking or cursing or they have not showered or taken ablution.

This means you cannot eat from any hotel or any restaurant. Because you do not know what kind of a person is cooking. You do not know the personality of the person cooking the food. Maybe he was making unbelief to God while he was cooking the food, or maybe he was not praying when he was cooking the food. That bad reflection that is on him or her and transfers to the food, then it is also reflected on you when you eat the food. And the food affects you on that seventh level.

And that is why saints always eat food that is not cooked. They often eat fruit, vegetables, olives that do not need anyone to make it. Or else they know they will not reach that level and they have to fall back from level seven—all the way back to the first level.

That is a big danger, and therefore you must know what is *ḥalāl* and what is *ḥarām*. It is not the *ḥalāl* and *ḥarām* that you are eating from Shariʿah, but from piety you want to adhere to the highest level of Shariʿah.

This means you have to know whether the water you are drinking was given to you by someone with ablution or not. If not, it can have a bad effect on you. And that is why many things affect saints. That is why they try as much as they can to use their own power to make food so that they will not be affected. For this reason you cannot eat any food if you are in need of a shower.[75] You cannot eat any food if you are not in ablution. You cannot force your wife to make food when she has her period; you have to cook for her and give her food. Because when she has her period God gave her excuse from praying. Since she is not able to pray, she cannot cook. You have to cook and give her food instead. Anyone who makes his wife cook for him when she is having her period, and eats from that food, he will be dropped from the eyes of saints.

---

[75] It is a requirement of *Shariʿah* to take a shower (*ghusl*) after having marital relations with one's spouse.

He has to go to the kitchen and cook, and offer food for the family. By this way he keeps himself and her clean from the reflection of the food that otherwise might affect him or her.

The Eighth Level—The Circle of Saints

Many people nowadays bring Hindus, or Buddhists or Zoroastrians into their houses as servants or helpers. We now are presenting Islam's rules, without discussing what people have to do. Any woman who brings someone to help her and takes off her scarf—if the lady who comes into her house does not believe in God, and is an idol worshipper or Zoroastrian (fire worshipper), or an atheist, then that woman is considered like a man, outside of her family, a non-*maḥram*. It is *ḥarām* to take her cover off.

Many people leave that practice of *Shariʿah*. It does not make you an unbeliever, but it is incorrect. You must ask for forgiveness, and God is forgiving.

Now that we have discussed that *Shariʿah* issue, we come back to discuss the discipline of *ṭarīqah.*

On the seventh level, you have to see who is cooking your food, who is ironing your clothes. Is that person on ablution or not? Is he keeping the faith? If he is not, that is worse. One Naqshbandi saint, Shah Bahauddin Naqshband, used to order his followers to take a shower. He had in his Sufi center a place where they could take a shower, and then they would put on very white clean clothes, because any clothes you wore and walked in the streets will carry bad energy. They had some people whose specialty was to clean and iron these clothes, and those people had to be on complete shower, in complete ablution, and while cleaning and ironing they could constantly ask God's forgiveness.

The followers who are wearing these clothes would immediately move from one room to another room to sit in *dhikr* so that the reflection from the outside would not be brought into the association of *dhikr*. This was to avoid the reflection of any bad energy—those reflections are a bad form of pollution even worse than the physical pollution from cars and factories.

They say that factories pollute nature. Human beings also make spiritual pollution which they spread to each other. And that is why for *dhikr*, for preparing food, for anything, you must be in perfect ablution from both sides. The one that is doing that action has to keep ablution twenty-four hours a day. And the other one who is offering the food or other work has to be in complete ablution. Both sides have to have complete ablution and complete forgiveness, in order to have a clean association, a clean meeting, where all spirits are present.

Prophet ﷺ sends his inspiration to such meetings, when everything is clean from both sides. That is level eight—if you keep that reciprocal discipline, meaning both in your person and in your worship and the one who is helping you with your worship by giving clothes, food, and what you need—are in ablution. Therefore the one providing these things is doing worship as well. So with those both sides you end up on level eight, the circle of spirits.

The level of the circle of spirits means that the saints come through their spirits and those that are in the association can feel their presence. That is why sometimes if a follower is doing his *dhikr* or seclusion, he may say at the end of the association, "Shaykh, can I ask a question?" Mawlana says, "Yes!" And he says, "Shaykh, I smelled a nice smell." Or another one might say, "Shaykh, it was as if someone was holding my hand." Or someone may say, "Oh, Shaykh, it was as if someone whispered in my ear, some praising of God." This is the circle of saints, and in the circle angels appear.

Angels come and that is the hadith of Prophet ﷺ:

> When a group of people sits together in a circle remembering their Lord, angels will come and encompass them and God's Mercy will come on them, and God mentions them in His Presence, in a Presence better than their presence.

So all this becomes something that you can experience on that eighth level. On that level everyone must be in complete obedience to the *sunnah* of Prophet Muhammad ﷺ. He has to follow it all or else he will not enter that level. He might interact with it. Sometimes he may notice a smell—a little here or a little there. But one does not perceive that completely until he is deeply following the *sunnah* of the Prophet ﷺ.

The shaykh never asks his follower to do something if the follower has not yet taken initiation and entered *ṭarīqah.* And if he has entered, the shaykh will ask him to do something to help in this way or that. On the other levels if the follower does not act on it, it means disrespect, but that inaction does not throw him back beyond step one.

But at level eight, when the follower begins to smell these smells and hear these voices and to interact with saints, then if the shaykh orders him to do something and he does not do it, he will not go back to the first level. He might even be thrown out of the Naqshbandi *ṭarīqah* and in his life he will never see the shaykh again. He might even go crazy.

One time a follower was trying hard, and he reached level eight. And there he was able to see. He saw the name of his shaykh on the Preserved Tablet—God had written that his shaykh was going to Hell.

He went back to himself and thought, "What am I seeing? Is this true that my shaykh is going to Hell? Is my shaykh doing something behind our backs we do not know? Can I see better than him now? Maybe my shaykh is not progressing... Maybe he is not progressing, only speaking. He is nothing and I have become better."

So that sickness came to his heart.

He loved his shaykh, so what he did he do? He went home and kept repeating, "O my Lord, forgive my shaykh, O my Lord, take my shaykh from Hellfire and put him in Paradise!" All the time in his prostration he was asking this, for forty days. After forty days he looked on the Preserved Tablet and he saw that his shaykh's name had changed from Hellfire to Paradise. He was so happy. As soon as he entered into the association of the shaykh, his shaykh was sitting in the middle and saw him coming.

He was happy to tell his Shaykh, "*Alḥamdulillāh*! I changed you from Hellfire to Paradise!"

As soon as he entered the presence of the shaykh, before he said anything, the shaykh took his *sunnah* tooth-stick (*miswāk*) and broke it. He said, "Unless you change me back to Hellfire, I am going to break you in half. Like this *miswak*, I am breaking you; go out from my presence. Put me back in Hellfire. I did not ask you to ask God to put me in Paradise. Bring me back to Hell. Make supplication to God until He turns my name back to Hellfire and then you can come back to my presence."

The follower was now afraid of the shaykh. He had thought that he was better than the shaykh, because he had changed him from Hellfire to Paradise!

So he went back, making prostration, prostration, and prostration, crying and crying for forty days until he looked at the Preserved Tablet again and saw that God had removed his shaykh's name from the list for Paradise and had put him back into Hellfire.

Very happily, he ran back to tell his Shaykh, "*Alḥamdulillāh*! O Shaykh Omar I am very happy you are in Hellfire now."

As soon as he came, his shaykh said, "O my son, for 25 years I saw that God had put me into Hellfire—I saw it on the Preserved Tablet. But my worship is not to escape Hellfire. I am not the Creator. I am God's servant. My job is to worship. If he puts me in Hellfire or in Paradise, that is up to Him. My job is to worship Him. We have no will. His Will is what is going to happen. We do what we have to do."

So on that eighth level, whatever the shaykh asked you is what you do. You do not do anything from yourself. Always your concentration is on what kind of order is coming from the shaykh, because that is the level of the Circle of Spirits, or Circle of Saints.

In that circle all communication is based on inspiration, there is nothing physical. Everything will be done from heart to heart. So whatever orders come are coming from a real source. There is a real source, to which you have to listen and obey. How did *Sayyīdinā*Muhammad ﷺ receive revelation from God through Jibril ﵇ ? He was listening and obeying. And what the Prophet ﷺ gave to his Companions, they listened and obeyed. Companions gave to saints, who in turn listened and obeyed. Saints give to their followers, who in their turn also listen and obey; listen and obey.

That is the level of saints where you have to listen and obey. That is the level where there are no questions. There is no "Why not?" You cannot ask, "Why is this not like that?" or "Why do we have to do it like that?" or "Why is this is better than that?" It is not up to you. It is up to the orders that come from above the shaykh; the shaykh has orders that come from above; grandshaykh to grandshaykh to grandshaykh to companions, originally coming from Prophet ﷺ.

At that level I am listening and obeying. If the shaykh say, "Take this, put it here!" Don't say no. You take it and put it. For example "Move this from here to here!" ... that is your job. You cannot disobey, if you disobey they throw you out. If they say to you, "Go!" you go. If they say to you, "Come" you come.

It is a sickness to think that you have become a big shaykh, when you are healing people.

There was a saint in Egypt recently; his name is Shaykh Muhammad Amīn al-Bagdhadi, Naqshbandi; this was 78 years ago. Most of the scholars at that time from the Middle East would go to Egypt to see him and to take initiation and study with him. And the shaykh gave some of them permission to conduct *dhikr* and bring people together. All of these shaykhs were scholars; he did not accept followers from normal people. His followers had to have been scholars for at least 13 years. To one of these followers he gave permission to conduct *dhikr*.

That student went back to his country, doing *dhikr* and promoting the Naqshbandi *ṭarīqat* and teaching people. More followers were coming and coming and coming. They began to say, "Masha-Allah, our shaykh is strong, our shaykh is strong, our shaykh is connected, our shaykh is his shaykh's representative!"

They were not talking about Shaykh Muhammad Amīn, but about the one conducting *dhikr* for him, Shaykh 'Abdu 'r-Raḥmān 'Azīz.

So people began to mention his name and he was beginning to put his name with the shaykh's name. When they read the Fātiḥa, they began to mention his name, and when they made supplication, they mentioned his name. As they began to mention his name more and more, that shaykh began to be happy with himself.

He forgot that it was the attraction of his shaykh that made him a shaykh.

If the shaykh wants to put your power out, you have nothing.

He began to say, and he told his followers, "You really do not know, the shaykh might want you to make meditation connection with me." As soon as he began to think like that and they followers began to recite Fātiḥa for him, and to make everything as if coming from him, he stopped telling them anything about the grandshaykh.

So the grandshaykh sent to his heart information, and he felt he needed to go visit him. So he did. During his visit he mentioned nothing of his students' making spiritual connection directly to him rather than to his shaykh, or of their putting his name with his shaykh's name, or of their reciting Fātiḥa with his name—he kept quiet. Before he left, he shook the shaykh's hand and said, "I am going." The shaykh said, "Go, I am changing your position now." He thought that he was getting a higher position.

He went back home; as soon as he landed, he immediately began to take his clothes off—he became crazy. For fifteen years he was crazy—not knowing how to say one word from his knowledge—it was finished. His shaykh took everything from his heart. So all these scholars and all his followers, from fifteen years, were going to the grandshaykh and asking him, "Please give back what you took, give him back his sanity. Make supplication for him so that God will bring him back."

When someone enters that level, he cannot make a mistake. No mistake is acceptable there. All these scholars were pleading, "*Yā Sayyīdī, Yā Sayyīdī,* please!" So in the end because of their pleading with him he said, "Ok, I am making supplication for him." As soon as he finished his supplication, saying "*Amīn*" and "*Fātiḥa,*" Shaykh ʿAbdu 'r-Raḥmān died.

That is level eight; once you put your foot there, no mistakes are permitted. Now if you make a mistake, not intentionally, its alright. If you make a mistake due to bad judgment, it is excusable. But if you make it, knowing that it is wrong, there is no excuse.

If you go deep inside Shariʿah, saints and scholars of Sufism are able to extract 500 obligations that the Prophet made clear for Companions and for the community—things that are required for us to do. There are other orders that are not obligatory, that if you leave them you are not in a sin but it is preferable to do them.

At level eight, you are obligated to do all 500 obligations and additionally all those things not deemed obligatory for ordinary Muslims—at that level you cannot leave any of them.

If you miss one, two, five, ten, it is alright, since they are not obligated. And you will understand this only through inspiration.

And the forbidden actions are 800. You have to leave them, and in saints' eyes if you leave one forbidden action for God's ﷻ sake, He rewards you as if you had done the 500 obligations. God willing, I will continue next time.

Migration is a One-Way Trip: the Discipline of Naqshbandiyya Begins Here

Insha-Allah we continue our explanation of the nine different disciplines that someone who enters this way must accomplish. We know it is very difficult, but we must at least make the intention.

As Prophet Muhammad ﷺ said:

> O people! The reward of deeds depends upon the intentions, and every person will get the reward according to what he has intended. So, whoever emigrated for Allah and His Apostle, then his emigration was for Allah and His Apostle, and whoever emigrated to take worldly benefit or for a woman to marry, then his emigration was for what he emigrated for.

When your intention is to migrate from one place to another for God and His Prophet ﷺ, then you will find God and His Prophet ﷺ. If you direct your face toward worldly things or to

Satan, then you are going to find that. It depends on your intention.

What is your intention? God will either reward or punish you. If you are thinking and seeking in the way of God, then for sure, even if your actions are insufficient—God will save you, He will bestow His Mercy on you and take you to your final destination.

There is a hadith from the Prophet ﷺ about two men. One was a servant all his life—worshiping, worshiping, worshiping—and the other was a normal person, making sins, repenting, making sins, repenting.

God's Will must happen. One day the good servant said, "I have spent all my life in worship. Never did I see worldly things, never did I enjoy myself in this life; I want to go one day and see this world that my brother is enjoying; I also want to enjoy it." So he moved from his cave to the city to enjoy worldly things.

At the same time, it came to the heart of the brother, who had enjoyed the world all his life, that it had been too long now—"I have been wasting my time; I am enjoying and enjoying; and now I want to repent. I will go to my brother in the cave and be like him and be with him. I want to leave worldly things. I will ask God's forgiveness."

So both of them moved, one toward worldliness and the other toward worship. While making their journeys, they both died. Angels came down to take their souls saying, "What to do with these two?"

The good servant's intention was to come to worldliness, so where should they take him? To Hell or to Paradise? And the one enjoying worldliness was trying to improve, seeking God's forgiveness. Where should they take him?

God inspired the angels to measure the distance that both of them had moved. If the distance of the servant is more than half of the way towards the city, take him to Hell; but if less, take him to Paradise. They measured the distance from each one to his destination to see for each one, if he was closer to the life of servanthood then he would be sent to Paradise. If he was closer to a life of corruption, he was sent to Hell.

All depends on your intention; you might spend your whole life running here and there, but at the end if you repent, God will forgive you."

My Mercy encompasses everything.[76]

The Prophet ﷺ related:

> When Allah created the Creation, He wrote in His Book--and He wrote (that) about Himself, and it is placed with Him on the Throne—"Verily My mercy overcomes My anger."[77]

So the nine good manners in this series of the Naqshbandi Order of good manners begin with the level of migration.

This means migration from worldliness to caring and preparing for the next world, from bad to good, from evil actions to better ones. You have to know that there is no hope in worldliness, the only hope is the next life.

We are not speaking here to students in school—we do not wish to discourage their study to become doctors or engineers. We are not discussing that issue; those students must go and live their lives; they have to study, learn, work; they have to act [according to the needs of this world and its interaction]. But we are speaking on the spiritual side, on the Islamic side about what they have to do in their lives [to develop] on a spiritual level.

Migration means to forget completely about worldliness, making your aim and goal God and Prophet Muhammad ﷺ.

---

[76] Sūratu ' l-ʿArāf (the Heights), 7:156.
[77] Bukhari.

Sayyidinā 'Alī ؓ said:

Prepare for this life as if you will live forever and prepare for your afterlife as if you will die tomorrow.

He also said:

Prepare for the next life in accordance with the amount of time you will spend there, and prepare for this life in accordance with the amount of time you will spend here.

So if you compare how much you are going to live in this world to how much you are going to live in your afterlife, this world comes to nothing, zero.

Therefore—this study of the nine levels of migration tells you that whatever you collect in this world is going to disappear.

Take cars, for example. I know some people who have more than 300 cars in their compounds. Have you seen that? I have. And every car is very expensive. They have perhaps 400 high class, $1,000,000 (or more) cars sitting in their garages. Nice cars. They have millions of dollars in the bank; they own ships and airplanes.

But what is the benefit? They are going to die. We are all going to die. They are going to leave everything. We, who own less, are not going to lose anything. But after our deaths we will be the same. After death, in spite of the difference between our wealth and theirs, they become like us and we become like them. Whoever in this world is migrating towards his Lord and his Prophet ﷺ is going to be in a better position after death.

That said, if God gives people wealth and they give it in His way, it is good. God is happy with the "thankful rich" who give in His way. A "thankful rich" person does not turn anyone away. If anyone comes and asks, "Give me from what God gave you!" then he will say, "yes, take!" and he gives. That is no problem. That person is from the "thankful rich," and God will reward him.

He is doing for the sake of God and His Prophet ﷺ sake; that is acceptable.

When you have a pain in your body, how do you feel? You may have a fever, and headaches, and your entire body may feel as though ants are moving through it—from bottom to top! This means that the body feels both excitement and sadness. The body feels pleasure and suffering. Some people have pain in the hands or feet only, but when the flu comes you may feel pain throughout your entire body. This means that every part of your body has a responsibility towards pleasure or suffering. Every cell—wherever there is a muscle, nerve, or vein—will experience pleasure or suffering.

When you decide to go in God's way, and to make migration for His Sake, it means that you cannot return to your starting point. When the Prophet ﷺ moved from Mecca to Medina, he did not go back to Mecca to establish his house. No, that time was finished!

Mecca was his birthplace, and the location of the House of God. But the Prophet went to Mecca only for pilgrimage and then returned to his home in Medina. So the meaning of migration is to go to one place, leaving another behind—forever. When you decide on migration, you cannot go back.

So when you begin on the nine levels of discipline, and move in the way of God and the Path of seekers, and take initiation from your shaykh, and move within the nine levels, then you have no right to move back towards your starting point. You have to continue.

If you step back one foot, the Prophet ﷺ will kick you out of his presence. From whatever level, 8 or 7 or 9 or 6—he will say, "This is the last point you reached." If you lose there, saints will dump on you all kinds of miseries that you will suffer all your life.

All these sufferings will end when you are dying and giving your last breath.

Then you are in the utmost need to be the presence of *Sayyīdinā* Muhammad ﷺ and your shaykh, in order that your soul will go easily from your body. If Prophet ﷺ and your shaykh do not appear there, it means you are losing the intercession of *Sayyīdinā* Muhammad ﷺ—you will be ending in pain and suffering.

Some weak-hearted people ask, "How do you know that?" It is not that I know it; my shaykh knows it, and his shaykh knows it. It is from heart to heart, back, back, , back all the way to the Prophet ﷺ. Those who believe will succeed. Those who do not believe, it is their problem. As soon as the follower takes initiation from the shaykh, there are lots of miraculous powers he can see coming from that light of his shaykh.

Don't think that the shaykh is blind and deaf. The shaykh feels himself to be the weakest servant, but God and His Prophet ﷺ gave him power. With that power they guide their followers. If an ant is moving on a stone, do you hear its voice or footsteps? No! But a shaykh can hear the footsteps of the ants if he is in the east and the ants are in the west. God can make him hear the ant's footsteps as we hear thunder. Don't think that the shaykh fails to hear what you are doing daily. God gave him that power from the hadith *qudsī* of the Prophet ﷺ, as God said:

> When My servant approaches Me through voluntary worship, I will love him. If I love him I will be his ears that he can hear with; I will be the eyes that he can see with; I will be the hand with which he acts and I will be the legs with which he walks."[78]

---

[78] Bukhari.

This means that God gave him power to hear what others cannot hear; to see what others cannot see; to say what people cannot say; to sense what people cannot sense; to walk in places people cannot reach.

That is a grant from God. It is not something that is hidden in Islam. Prophet Muhammad ﷺ mentioned it. God gave it to saints. So the shaykh is not blind. God gives him vision. He can see his follower even in China, or if he is in Indonesia to his followers in America. He can appear to his follower. He can speak with his follower. Even if his follower is far away, he can reach him. And the follower says, "O, what you are doing here, my Shaykh, when did you arrive, when did you travel, with what did you come?" He does not say anything, only "*Salām*!" and goes.

So when you migrate from one level to another level, you cannot go back to where you were before or you will be thrown out and you will not receive the intercession of Prophet Muhammad ﷺ, because your shaykh will be unhappy with you. Therefore, when you give initiation and you reach a level, you have to know that there is no more playing. No more childish actions! You are responsible for what you are doing. At that level of seeking and reaching among those nine levels, you will see the presence of all saints around you. You will sense them, will smell their smell and sometimes will see them. Not with your heart's eyes, but your physical eyes. You will see them and speak with them.

Being in that kind of physical awareness of them, you have to imagine how difficult it is to appear before them with dirty clothes. You have to clean yourself to be in their presence. And the process of cleaning is not like cleaning your clothes—it is cleaning the spiritual clothing of your body.

How is it that you feel as if ants are moving throughout your body if you have, for example, a fever? Do you feel them (ants) in every cell of your body? You have to feel that every cell of your body is in mistakes, in sins, and now is moving away from the level of sin; like an ant migrating towards God and His Prophet ﷺ.

Take the example previously mentioned of the two brothers, one a servant and the other a worldly man—one moving away from the world to the life of the afterlife, and the angels measuring his progress in his journey. If he has completed fifty percent or more of his journey he goes to Paradise. You have to know that angels are measuring in every moment the distance that your body's cells are improving themselves or deteriorating.

Sometimes you wake up from a dream—that dream could be a nice dream or one that makes you afraid. But whatever dream it was, it was intense and you feel that your hair is standing on end. You feel it throughout your entire body. If you touch any place on your body, you feel your skin is standing up; you have goose bumps everywhere. Standing up, afraid! So every cell in your body must be, at every moment, progressing through these nine levels—as responsive to these nine levels as they are to your dreams—standing and showing their belief in their Lord's Oneness.

They must be saying, "*Lā ilāha illa-Llāh, Muḥammadun rasūlullāh*!" ﷺ Every cell of your body must be stirred—as it can be aroused during a (good or bad) dream, or by pleasure, or by fear. Each cell must be standing—that cell speaks up and says, "*Lā ilāha illa-Llāh, Muḥammadun rasūlullāh*!" ﷺ. Your entire system must be saying this, and declaring its piety in understanding and acceptance that Prophet Muhammad ﷺ is the symbol of creation; is the creation; is the servant of God and is responsible towards the whole of creation for God.

When the cells of this body get goose bumps, he has to know that every cell of his body is asking repentance and saying, "O my Lord, you created me, brought me from nothing into existence. I came into existence and You ordered me (on the Day of Promises) to do what You wanted me to do of obligations, but I came into this world doing nothing but sins. I left your orders. I did not do anything. I became disobedient to You and to Your Prophet ﷺ. I was disobedient to saints, and to my parents; I was disobedient to everything, and I am obedient only to my ego.

"O God, forgive me! You have brought me from complete nothingness."

Complete nothingness means you cannot see anything. Only God only knows what is there. It is His creation.

"You brought me from complete nothingness into existence, and asked me to carry the trust. O God, You asked the heavens, earth, and mountains to carry your trust, but they feared to take it, saying, 'O our Lord, it is difficult!' But we human beings were very happy to carry it, and we are ignorant and oppressors to ourselves. O my Lord! Forgive me my ignorance and my oppression of others. I repent from whatever you asked me to do on the Day of Promises and then left during my time in this world—I did nothing except sin. I repent. I am a weak servant."

You have to know that every cell can stand and become good; can feel the ant movement and the pleasure; this means they can say what we are saying now and you have to hear it and understand that your body is asking forgiveness from God. If you cannot hear it, that means you are still at the level of childishness. As you are moving along the way and your body is in complete daily repentance through its whole self, God will order these cells to move and concentrate their energy into your heart. That energy becomes one concentrated center in the heart, into which God will send His Light, and that is why God said to the Prophet ﷺ:

> Neither My heavens or My earth contains Me, but the heart of the believer contains Me.

So as soon as all this energy moves, as they repent and repent and repent, God accepts. With the power of the shaykh, and his requesting by means of the Prophet ﷺ, God moves that power to the heart. And as it moves to the heart, it can receive God's Light. Then God will bestow His Light and His Attributes—the Beautiful Names—into the heart of that seeker.

THE NINTH LEVEL—*DHIKR* OF THE CAVE TAUGHT BY *SAYYIDINA* ABU BAKR

As Prophet ﷺ migrated from Mecca to Medina in the company of Abū Bakr aṣ-Ṣiddīq ؓ, you are following in their footsteps to migrate with your shaykh from bad desires of your life to the highest utmost good desires for the afterlife. During that migration the Prophet ﷺ, along with *Sayyīdinā* Abū Bakr aṣ-Ṣiddīq ؓ went to the cave.

The unbelievers were going to capture the Prophet ﷺ or kill him. However since he ﷺ is the Messenger of God, no one could touch him. Why did he go to that cave? Saints say it was in order to give his secrets to *Sayyīdinā* Abū Bakr aṣ-Ṣiddīq ؓ. From his heart to the heart of *Sayyīdinā* Abū Bakr aṣ-Ṣiddīq ؓ. And *Sayyīdinā* Abū Bakr aṣ-Ṣiddīq ؓ then called all the atoms and spirits of Naqshbandi followers; because Naqshbandis take from Abū Bakr aṣ-Ṣiddīq ؓ directly.

Sayyīdinā Abū Bakr aṣ-Ṣiddīq ؓ called all the spirits of the Naqshbandis, and called upon Imam ʿAbdu 'l-Khāliq al-Ghujdawānī ق. Then *Sayyīdinā* Abū Bakr aṣ-Ṣiddīq ؓ taught Imam ʿAbdu 'l-Khāliq al-Ghujdawānī ق the group *dhikr* of Naqshbandis, and Imam ʿAbdu 'l-Khāliq al-Ghujdawānī ق lead all the Naqshbandis in *dhikr*.

For that reason, on the ninth level the follower has no right to leave the Naqshbandi *dhikr*—he must participate every week. He has to do the long one once a week. The short one he must do every day. Nowadays, every week we do the small one, because people cannot carry too much worship. So saints make it easy on us, so we do a small group *dhikr* every week, where originally you had to do the long one once a week and the short one once a day.

The importance of the Naqshbandi group *dhikr* is that it was taught during the migration of Prophet Muhammad ﷺ from Mecca to Medina. It was taught originally by *Sayyīdinā* Abū Bakr aṣ-Ṣiddīq ؓ. So missing the Naqshbandi group *dhikr* without an excuse is a very grave action in the Naqshbandi order that might be dangerous for you and will throw you out of the presence of saints.

If you cannot come to the group *dhikr*, then you can do it at home by yourself. It is an obligation that everyone has to do it, and the one that has an excuse can do it at home. A person can have an excuse. If he is sick, no problem! If he has important guest that he cannot bring to *dhikr*, and has to spend time with them, it is considered that he has an excuse.

If someone offered him three golden coins to come to a meeting and he goes to that other meeting for the coins, then he has no excuse for not coming to the Naqshbandi group *dhikr*. Three golden coins, how much are they worth? $300. So if you go to a meeting for $300, you have no excuse for missing *dhikr*. If someone tells you, "This is $300, come to group *dhikr*," then there is an obligation on you to come, you have no excuse for not coming without taking anything. And if your shaykh says "I give you $300 rupees to come to *dhikr*" and you say, "O my shaykh, I am sick, or I am busy with important guests, I cannot come!" At that time you have an excuse worth 300 dollars.

Why then are people not coming for the *dhikr*? They are busy with worldly things. Be careful from the Angel of Death, Azrāʿīl ؑ. He does not ask them how much money they made. He is sometimes easy and sometimes very tough. For believers, he takes their soul like you take the hair from grease. For wrongdoers, O my God—all kinds of punishment comes upon them.

What kind of punishment is being given in this time? Today there are suicide bombers, people burning in fire, people burned by rockets blowing them to pieces. Compared to what comes on unbelievers, that is easy. So what kind of punishment will He send on people? You cannot put it into words. How many cells are there in the body? Three trillion cells. Trillions. More than millions, more than billions. For those being punished every cell is going to suffer.

The First Khatm Khwajagan

When the Prophet ﷺ migrated from Mecca to Madinah, he was ordered to pass by a cave. According to Shariʿah, that cave was called Gharu Thawr and is one day's distance from Mecca. The Prophet ﷺ stayed there three days. Why did the Prophet ﷺ stay in that cave? He was able to continue. There is a secret that caused him stop in that cave.

The Prophet ﷺ was ordered to migrate from Mecca to Madinah for the purpose of going inside the cave Gharu Thawr. That is where God taught him how to make *dhikr*.[79] It was the first time that the Prophet ﷺ, made *dhikr* with a loud voice. That is a very great Sufi secret indeed.

Migration from Mecca to Madinah was very easy for the Prophet ﷺ. He had only to say *"Bismi'l-Lāhi 'r-Raḥmāni 'r-Raḥīm"* and he was in Madinah; just as it was easy for him to take sand from the ground and throw it in the faces of the ignorant people and they were unable to see him as he was going out of his house. Or he could have ridden and reached Madinah in ten or fifteen days. Why did he go to that cave the "Cave of Silent Secrets"? Since no one knew about this—why was Prophet ﷺ ordered by God to go to that cave, which is one day away from Mecca, when he had a distance of fifteen days travel to go?

---

[79] *Dhikr*: any invocation of the Names of God or declaration of sacred phrases (*kalimatu ṭayyibah*), inwardly or outwardly, spontaneously or repetitiously, individually or collectively.

When the Prophet ﷺ went into that cave the spider and the pigeon came and made a house over the door in order that no one would know what is inside. This is the common knowledge from the *sīrah*. As for the secret, look to love. When love for someone is pure, God will never forget that person. Before leaving Mecca for Madinah, the Prophet ﷺ put someone in his bed because the people of ignorance came to his door intent on killing him. He put *Sayyidinā* ʿAlī ؓ in his bed. This means that he made *Sayyidinā* ʿAlī ؓ his representative. He did not put anyone of the Sahaba, except someone of his own flesh and blood. And he took with him as company that other reflection of himself, *Sayyidinā* Abū Bakr, to the cave. He said:

> I am the city of knowledge and ʿAlī is the door.[80]

The door is something physical, external. When you want to enter the house here, how do you enter? Through the door. In order to enter to the Prophet ﷺ and to come to the knowledge that the Prophet ﷺ is giving, you have to enter through the door. That door was *Sayyidinā* ʿAlī ؓ. And the Prophet ﷺ also said:

> Whatever God has poured into my heart I poured into the heart of Abū Bakr aṣ-Ṣiddīq.[81]

The Prophet ﷺ referred to the secret of Abū Bakr ؓ also when he said:

> Abū Bakr does not surpass you for fasting or praying more but because of a secret that took root in his heart.[82]

So inside the house is *Sayyidinā* Abū Bakr ؓ and outside the house, we find *Sayyidinā* ʿAlī ؓ. That is why, of the two Sufi knowledges, one came from *Sayyidinā* Abū Bakr and one from

---

80 At-Tirmidhī. Al-Ḥākim, Ibn ʿAsākir, al-ʿIrāqī, al-Haythamī, as-Suyūṭī.
81 Maybūdī, Rāzī, as-Suyūṭī.
82 Aḥmad al-Ghazālī, al-Ḥākim.

Sayyidinā 'Alī ☙. From the time of the four *madhāhib*,[83] Muslims have thought that the knowledge of the heart came from these two paths. Justice and laws, on the other hand, came from *Sayyidinā* 'Umar ☙.

The Prophet's ﷺ saying about Abū Bakr is the secret of the cave. To represent his physicality, the Prophet ﷺ put *Sayyidinā* 'Alī ☙ in his bed prior to his departure Mecca to Madinah. This means that *Sayyidinā* 'Alī ☙ was used for the outside. But to the cave he took with him *Sayyidinā* Abū Bakr ☙. For the cave represents what is interior. In Qur'an, God is ordering us:

> *Enter, resort to the cave! Your Lord will shower His mercies on you and dispose of your affair towards comfort and ease.* [84]

And who is the cave for this Nation except the Prophet ﷺ? It is an order for everyone on this earth to run to the cave, and everyone has a cave in his heart which directs you to the big cave, the general cave, and that is the heart of the Prophet ﷺ, and that big cave takes you to the mercy of your Lord.

Who did *Sayyidinā* Muhammad ﷺ choose to go with him to the cave? It was *Sayyidinā* Abū Bakr aṣ-Ṣiddīq ☙. When the Prophet ﷺ entered the cave, he was very tired. He reclined and placed his head on Abū Bakr aṣ-Ṣiddīq's leg. Who, I ask, can put the head of a prophet over his leg? *Sayyidinā* Abū Bakr aṣ-Ṣiddīq ☙ bore on his leg the head of the most Beloved One of Allah. This is a big honor for *Sayyidinā* Abū Bakr aṣ-Ṣiddīq ☙ that the Prophet Muhammad ﷺ has put his honorable head on his leg. For us the Prophet ﷺ was sleeping, but for him, it was Mi'raj or ascension. He knows no sleep:

> My eyes sleep but my heart never sleeps.[85]

---

[83] Arabic: *madhāhib*: the major schools of legal thought in Islam: Māliki, Shāfi'ī, Ḥanafī, Hanbalī.
[84] Sūratu 'l-Kahf (the Cave), 18:16.

His heart never sleeps! His heart is always connected with his Lord. He is always in ascension.

I once heard this from my Shaykh who, in turn, heard it from his Grandshaykh: People say that the Prophet ﷺ went to his Lord in the Night Journey. According to Naqshbandi teachings and secrets which they took from the heart of *Sayyidinā* Abū Bakr aṣ-Ṣiddīq, there were twelve thousand night–journeys for the Prophet ﷺ in his life, not just one. He is always in ascension, always with his Lord. He went to the Divine Presence.

He was at a distance of two bow-lengths or nearer[86]

He came very close. "How" is not our business—Allah and the Prophet ﷺ know because he reached that place. No one can know that level. Even the Archangel Gabriel was not able to know, because he said, "I cannot pass my level" when the Prophet ﷺ was telling him to continue with him. "If I go further, I will be burnt."

The teachings of Naqshbandis and *awlīyā* of *Sayyidinā* Muḥīyiddīn Ibn 'Arabī, *Sayyidinā* 'Abda 'l-Qādir al-Gilānī, and all the Sufis say that Archangel Gabriel should have moved forward with the Prophet ﷺ even if he was going to be burnt. As the Prophet ﷺ said to Archangel Gabriel, "I am going to move even if I am going to be burnt." He sacrificed himself to get that light for his nation by saying: "I have no concern for myself." That is why he was moving forward, constantly progressing, traveling to that level where he came very close to his Lord.

At that time God asked him, "Who are you?" What do you think the Prophet ﷺ is going to answer? Is there a "Muhammad" there, is there "a prophet" there, in the presence of his Lord? Who can be something in the Presence of Allah? So he said, "O my

---

[85] Bukhari and Muslim.

[86] Sūratu 'n-Najm (the Star), 53:9.

Lord, I am not seeing myself. I am not seeing anything except You. There is no one except You."

That secret, the Prophet ﷺ wished to pass on to *Sayyidinā* Abū Bakr aṣ-Ṣiddīq ؓ. Thus, he took him to the cave. He could have taken *Sayyidinā* ʿAlī ؓ or *Sayyidinā* ʿUmar ؓ or four people but he only took one. But he took someone about whom he said: "Whatever my Lord has put in my heart I put in the heart of Abū Bakr aṣ-Ṣiddīq."

So, as the Prophet ﷺ was lying down, his head on the leg of *Sayyidinā* Abū Bakr aṣ-Ṣiddīq ؓ, Abū Bakr saw a hole in the wall of the cave and *Sayyidinā* Abū Bakr ؓ put his foot against the hole to close it. He began to feel something biting him and felt great pain. He was feeling as if he was losing his body. He was trying to control himself, until the flesh of his foot was eaten half away. As his flesh was being eaten, a large snake reared its head. *Sayyidinā* Abū Bakr aṣ-Ṣiddīq ؓ began to cry and a tear fell on the Prophet's ﷺ face. The Prophet ﷺ said, "Oh Abū Bakr! Why are you crying? Do not be sad: God is with us![87]

The Prophet's ﷺ question also contains a teaching, because he knows. "Are you afraid, he asked Abū Bakr ؓ, that people are going to come and kill us?" Abū Bakr said, "*Yā Rasūlullāh,* I am not crying for fear that they will kill me; I am not afraid of them. But I am crying because of a snake which is eating my foot. When he finishes with me, he will be coming to you, and I was afraid for you. My heart's blood was burning for you and that is why I cried." The Prophet ﷺ spoke with the snake and said: "Don't you know that the flesh of prophets is forbidden for you to eat, and the flesh of the veracious saints is also forbidden?" The snake answered, "O Messenger of God, when my Lord created me I knew about you before you were created in this world through

[87] Sūratu 't-Tawbah (Repentance), 9:40.

your mother's womb, and I asked my Lord forty thousand years ago to keep me alive to see your face and then die. Now *Sayyidinā* Abū Bakr aṣ-Ṣiddīq is blocking my view with his feet. I have to see you and fulfill my Lord's promise and he is blocking the hole with his feet. That is why I was obliged to eat and come through the hole in order to be able to look at you."

It is said: "The saliva of a believer is a cure."[88]

So the Prophet said, *"Bismi'l-Lāhi 'r-Raḥmāni 'r-Raḥīm,"* and applied his saliva to the foot of Abū Bakr and the foot was immediately healed and whole as before. Then the Prophet ordered the snake to look at him. The snake said, "I believe that there is but One God, and I believe that you are Muhammad, His Prophet."

And the snake was coming and turning in circles... Grandshaykh said, according to *Sayyidinā* 'Alī's and *Sayyidinā* Abū Bakr's inspirations, that snake was going around and around for two hours, looking at the Prophet's face. After it looked, the Prophet said, "Now what you have asked from your Lord is fulfilled; now, die." That snake died and immediately disappeared. That incident was a test for *Sayyidinā* Abū Bakr aṣ-Ṣiddīq to see if he was going to protect the Prophet or not—was he going to be afraid for himself or for the Prophet? But he sacrificed himself for the sake of the Prophet.

That was a snake, an animal; what about us? We are not believing, we are denying. To be sure, we are denying. We are believing with our tongues but in our hearts we are denying. We are fighting with one another. And when we fight with each

---

[88] This saying is not raised to the status of hadith but according to the scholars of traditions (*muḥaddithīn*) the meaning is true based on the hadith of Ibn 'Abbās from ad-Darqutnī's *Afrād*, "Among the acts of humility is the man who drinks the left over of his brother."

other, that's it! We are denying Allah; we are denying the Prophet ﷺ.

In that sacred, holy cave, God ordered the Prophet ﷺ to pass whatever secrets God had ordered to give, up to a point known to Him, to the heart of *Sayyidinā* Abū Bakr aṣ-Ṣiddīq ؓ. The Prophet ﷺ then passed the secret of his knowledge. That is why this hadith came from *Sayyidinā* Abū Hurayrah ؓ:

> I have retained from the Prophet ﷺ two vessels of knowledge. One knowledge I have disseminated among people; but if I tell the other knowledge, they will cut my throat.[89]

That is hidden knowledge, *'ilmun min Ladunni.* That knowledge is in the heart only, it can never be written down. No one can carry this knowledge. That is the knowledge that the Prophet ﷺ put in the heart of *Sayyidinā* Abū Bakr aṣ-Ṣiddīq ؓ.[90]

If *Sayyidinā* Abū Bakr aṣ-Ṣiddīq ؓ was going to disseminate that knowledge, Allah knows what they would have said about him—they would have cut his throat. So he hid it. But he passed it on to his successor, *Sayyidinā* Salmān al-Fārsī ؓ. Then *Sayyidinā* Salmān ؓ passed it to *Sayyidinā* Qāsim ؓ, the son of *Sayyidinā* Abū Bakr ؓ, then *Sayyidinā* Qāsim ؓ passed it to *Sayyidinā* J'afar aṣ-Ṣādiq ؓ, the Sixth Imam. That secret was passed from one to another, from one to another, from heart to heart, until it reached

---

[89] Bukhari.

[90] Imam Qastalānī relates in his *al-Mawāhib* that on the night of the Ascension the Holy Prophet said, "My Lord revealed to me three different types of knowledge, he told me not to reveal the first to anyone because none but I can understand it. He said you may communicate the second science to whom you wish and teach the third to all of your Community."

Mawlana Khālid al-Baghdādī. That Golden Chain[91] begins from the Prophet ﷺ, goes to *Sayyidinā* Abū Bakr aṣ-Ṣiddīq ؓ, and then down to Mawlana Khālid al-Baghdādī ق, who is buried in Damascus. Then Mawlana Khālid spread it in a huge way between East and West by having three-hundred Caliphs so that this knowledge reached everywhere. That is the origin of the Most Sublime Naqshbandi Order; it began in that cave.

All Sufi orders come from that cave. Someone was reciting the verse of God giving His hand under the tree:

Those who swear their loyalty to you swear their loyalty to God; God's hand is over their hand.[92]

This is the open meaning in the Qur'an. The secret meaning is that God ordered the Prophet ﷺ, "O my beloved Muhammad ﷺ, now order all saints to come to your presence." And the Prophet ﷺ immediately ordered Abū Bakr aṣ-Ṣiddīq ؓ and *Sayyidinā* ʿAlī ؓ who was present spiritually, to bring all saints who had taken secrets from *Sayyidinā* ʿAlī ؓ or *Sayyidinā* Abū Bakr ؓ to be present in that cave. At that time, 124,000 saints were ready spiritually—even though they had not been created in this world yet, they were present spiritually. And the Prophet ﷺ said to each saint: "Whatever followers you have, whom God gave you on the Day of Promises, call them spiritually." Everyone was called spiritually to the presence of the Prophet ﷺ in that cave. All of us sitting here, all the Sufi groups wherever they are, it is enough for them to call themselves "Sufi"—they were in the presence of the Prophet ﷺ in that cave. They were present spiritually.

Then God commanded the Prophet ﷺ to order each saint to put his hand over the hand of his disciples to initiate them and all

[91] The Golden Chain: the *silsilah* or chain of Khwajagān or spiritual masters of the Naqshbandi-Haqqani Sufi path. This chain culminates with Mawlana Shaykh Muhammad Nazim al-Haqqani, who is its fortieth link.

[92] Sūratu 'l-Fatḥ (the Opening), 48:10.

disciples were putting their hand under the hand of their saints. The Prophet ﷺ ordered *Sayyidinā* ʿAlī to put his hand over all the forty *ṭarīqah* (Sufi paths) that issue from him and ordered *Sayyidinā* Abū Bakr aṣ-Ṣiddīq ؓ to put his hand over the *ṭarīqah* Naqshbandīyyah, the Ṣiddīqīyyah *Ṭarīqah.* While today it is called Naqshbandīyya, but before, in his time it was known as the Ṣiddīqīyyah, and after that it was called Ṭayfūrīyya, Ghujdwānīyya, and so on, on the name of the *walī* it was under at the time. So after Grandshaykh that lineage from Grandshaykh [going back] to Abū Bakr aṣ-Ṣiddīq, to the Prophet ﷺ it is called Naqshbandi-Ḥaqqānīyya, after our master Mawlana Shaykh Nazim.

Then the Prophet ﷺ put his hand over *Sayyidinā* ʿAlī and *Sayyidinā* Abū Bakr aṣ-Ṣiddīq ؓ, and God put His hand over them and recited that verse Himself:

> *Those who receive initiation from you receive initiation from God; God's hand is over their hands; whoever gives back his initiation, he is going to lose; and whoever keeps the promise that he made to God, God will keep that person.*[93]

Immediately, all of us—all forty Sufi paths and the Naqshbandi Path were saying in one sound, with one voice,

Allāhū Allāhū Allāhū Ḥaqq

Allāhū Allāhū Allāhū Ḥaqq

Allāhū Allāhū Allāhū Ḥaqq

three times, according to God's own wording and all of us were hearing God's own words as that secret was put into our own hearts. After that, Grandshaykh continued: "Anyone who was in that cave was going to be with the others in this life reciting *dhikr*, and anyone who recites *dhikr* must know that he was in the cave

---

[93] Sūratu 'l-Faṭh (the Opening), 48:10.

with the Prophet ﷺ, with *Sayyidinā* 'Alī ؓ, with *Sayyidinā* Abū Bakr ؓ and with all the saints."

The Prophet ﷺ ordered that all prophets and *awlīyāullāh* should be there in spirit, and *Sayyidinā* 'Abdul Khāliq al-Ghujdawānī ق after whom the Khatm al-Khwajagān received his name called all the *dharrāt,* the atoms of all who are in *ṭarīqah.*[94] And because we are Naqshbandi it means we were there under the *talqīn* of *Sayyidinā* Muhammad ﷺ and *Sayyidinā* Abū Bakr aṣ-Ṣiddīq ؓ . And it was put on the tongues of the people doing *dhikr,* "*Allāhū Allāhū Allāhū Ḥaqq.*"

That is evidence of the reward that you will be in every assocation taking place under the Naqshbandi Sufi order. That lineage, all its grandshaykhs were present and all their followers were present as well, and Shaykh 'Abdul Khāliq al-Ghujdawānī ق led the Khatm al-Khawajagān, under those *tajallīs* and under that reward. From that time they were under that *talqīn,* to put on your tongue what they are saying. If we say "*Allāhū Ḥaqq*" as they put on our tongue, imitating the way they are doing, in reality what they are putting is not in imitation, but are true teachings that your tongue begins to do it and recite it. From that time, that reward is moving until Judgment Day, on every one of us—on every Naqshbandi.

Allah ﷻ doesn't reject anyone who is asking. And the Prophet ﷺ was asking Allah ﷻ with all these *awlīyā,* and Allah ﷻ has sent that teaching to the Prophet ﷺ and the Prophet ﷺ to *Sayyidinā* 'Abdul Khāliq al-Ghujdawānī ق to teach the followers of this chain.

That is the *barakah* of *awlīyāullāh* how they do that and we cannot see it but the traces of the light that is in our heart are

---

[94] Arabic: *ṭarīqah* –the Sufi Path, the method of spiritual progress, the way to the knowledge of God.

always pulling us to the best. So when the level of *īmān*, faith, is going less and the level of Shaytan is increasing, that comes from our actions which are not acceptable. Then when our level of *īmān* increasing you realize you must repent and ask forgiveness and then as along as you keep your *īmān* strong it will increase your good actions, *'amal*.

As the Prophet ﷺ said "between two prayers there is forgiveness of sins." So if I pray Ẓuhr, then make some sins and then go pray 'Asr, Allah will take the sins away. But I am still on the same level. If I pray Ẓuhr[95] and don't make sins up to 'Asr, then my level is increasing. If I reach to Maghrib, at that level I will get more reward. I will get rewarded according to the level of *īmān* I am in. We don't want to bring the level of our *īmān* down, as between one prayer to the next prayer is *kaffārat adh-dhunūb*, forgiveness for sins. But if you are not making sins, then when you are praying you begin to progress; to have *kashf*, unveiling, and *ilhām*, all kinds of good inspirations coming to the heart.

There is not enough time now to mention them, but in that cave many, many secrets were bestowed upon the Sufi people who were following Sayyidinā 'Alī or *Sayyidinā* Abū Bakr aṣ-Ṣiddīq ؓ. And when the Prophet ﷺ the next day continued his migration from Mecca to Madinah, all of us, all the Sufi followers, were migrating after the Prophet ﷺ, with him, from Mecca to Madinah. That is why the people of *dhikr, adh-dhākirīn'Llāh*,[96] the people of Sufi paths, are with the Prophet ﷺ, migrating from Mecca to Madinah, and that reward is only for the Sufi groups. It is not given to anyone else.

When they reached Madinah, there were some people watching from the palm-trees to see if the Prophet ﷺ was coming. When those people saw the Prophet ﷺ and saw the spiritual

---

[95] Arabic: *Ẓuhr*: Midday; noon. One of the five obligatory prayers.
[96] Arabic: *adh-dhākirīn'Llāh*: those who remember God.

people coming after him, they began to praise the Prophet ﷺ in verse:

> *From the hill-tops of the South*
> *The full moon doth arise.*
> *With what a lovely call*
> *Unto God doth he call,*
> *And we thank him for it all.*
> *O you sent by the Merciful,*
> *You have come, best of heralds.*
> *You have honored Madinah,*
> *We bow to thy demand.*[97]

[97] From the *sīrah* (life of the Prophet ﷺ).

GLOSSARY

ʿabd (pl. *ʿIbād*): lit. slave, servant.

ʿAbd Allāh: Lit., "servant of God"

ʿAbd Allāh al-Fa'iz ad-Dāghestanī, Shaykh: 39th master of theNaqshbandi Golden Chain and Shaykh of Mawlana Shaykh Nazim.

ʿAbda 'l-Qādir al-Gilānī, Shaykh: known as the Ghawth, Arch-intercessor, he was the epynomous fouder of the Qādirī Sufi order.

ʿAbdul Khāliq al-Ghujdawānī, Khwājah: one of the masters of the Naqshbandi lineage and the leader of the Khatm al-Khawajagān.

Abū Bakr aṣ-Ṣiddīq ﷺ: one the closest Companions to the Prophet ﷺ, his father-in-law, who shared the Hijrah with him. After the Prophet's death, he was elected as the first caliph (successor) to the Prophet ﷺ. He is known as one of the most saintly of the Prophet's Companions.

Abū Yazīd/Bayāzīd Bistāmī: A great ninth century *walī* and master in the Naqshbandi Golden Chain.

adab: good manners, proper etiquette.

adhān: call to prayer.

al: Arabic definite article, "the"

ʿalamīn: world; universes.

alḥamdulillāh: Praise God.

ʿAlī ibn Abī Ṭālib ﷺ: the cousin of the Prophet ﷺ, married to his daughter Fāṭimah and fourth caliph of the Prophet ﷺ.

alif: first letter of Arabic alphabet ا.

ʿAlīm, al-: the Knower, a divine attribute

Allāh: proper name for God in Arabic.

Allāhu Akbar: God is Greater.

ʿamal: good deed (pl. *ʿamāl*).

amīr (pl., *umarā*): chief, leader, head of a nation or people.

anā: first person singular pronoun

anbīyā: prophets (sing. *nabī*).

ʿaql: intellect, reason; from the root *ʿaqila*, lit., "to fetter."

ʿArafah: a plain near Mecca where pilgrims gather for the principal rite of Hajj.

ʿarif: knower, gnostic; one who has reached spiritual knowledge of his Lord.

ʿārifūn' bi 'l-Lāh: knowers of God

ar-Raḥīm: The Mercy-Giving, Merciful, Munificent, one of Allah's ninety-nine Holy Names

ar-Raḥmān: The Most Merciful, Compassionate, Beneficent, the most often repeated of Allah's Holy Names.

ʿarsh, al-: Divine Throne

aṣl: root, origin, basis.

astaghfirullāh: lit. "I seek Allah's forgiveness."

awliyāullāh: saints of Allah (sing. *walī*).

āyah/āyāt (pl. Ayāt): a verse of the Holy Qur'an.

Āyat al-Kursī: the Verse of the Throne, a well-known verse from the Qur'an (2:255).

'Azrā'īl: the Archangel of Death.

Badī' al-: The Innovator; a Divine Name.

Banī Ādam: Children of Ādam; humanity.

Bayt al-Maqdis: the Sacred Mosque in Jerusalem, built at the site where Solomon's Temple was later erected.

Bayt al-Ma'mūr: much-frequented house; this refers to the Ka'bah of the heavens, which is the prototype of the Ka'bah on earth and is circumambulated by the angels.

baya': pledge; in the context of this book, the pledge of initiation of a disciple (*murid*) to a shaykh.

bismi'l-Lāhi 'r-Raḥmāni 'r-Raḥīm: "In the name of the All-Merciful, the Compassionate"; this is the introductory verse to all the chapters of the Qur'an except the ninth.

Dajjāl: the False Messiah (Antichrist) whom the Prophet ﷺ foretold as coming at the end-time of this world, who will deceive mankind with pretensions of being divine.

dalālah: evidence

dhāt: self / selfhood

dhawq (pl. adhwāq): tasting; technical term referring to the experiential aspect of gnosis.

dhikr: remembrance, mention of God through His Holy Names or phrases of glorification.

ḍīyā: light.

Diwān al-Awlīyā: the gathering of saints with the Prophet ﷺ in the spiritual realm. This takes place every night.

du'a: supplication.

dunyā: world; worldly life.

'eid: festival; the two major festivals of Islam are 'Eid al-Fitr, marking the completion of Ramadan, and 'Eid al-Adha, the Festival of Sacrifice during the time of Hajj.

farḍ: obligatory worship.

Fātiḥah: Sūratu 'l-Fātiḥah; the opening chapter of the Qur'an.

Ghafūr, al-: The Forgiver; a Divine Name.

ghawth: lit. "Helper"; the highest ranking saint the in hierarchy of saints.

ghaybu' l-muṭlaq, al-: the absolute unknown, known only to God.

ghusl: full shower/bath obligated by a state of ritual impurity prior to worship.

Grandshaykh: generally, a *walī* of great stature. In this text, where spelled with a capital G, "Grandshaykh" refers to Mawlana 'Abd Allāh ad-

Daghestani (d. 1973), Mawlana Shaykh Nazim's master.

hā': letter ه

ḥadīth nabawī (pl., ahadith): prophetic hadith whose meaning and linguistic expression are those of the Prophet Muḥammad ﷺ.

ḥadith qudsī: divine saying whose meaning directly reflects the meaning God intended but whose linguistic expression is not Divine Speech as in the Qur'an, it thus differs from a hadith *nabawī* (*see* above).

ḥaḍr: present

ḥaywān: animal.

ḥajj: the sacred pilgrimage of Islam obligatory on every mature Muslim once in his/her life.

ḥalāl: permitted, lawful according to the Islamic Shariʿah.

ḥaqīqah, al-: reality of existence; ultimate truth.

ḥaqq: truth

Ḥaqq, al-: the Divine Reality, one of the 99 Divine Names.

ḥarām: forbidden, unlawful.

hāshā: God forbid!

ḥarf: (pl. *ḥurūf*) letter; Arabic root "edge."

Ḥawā: Eve.

hijrah: emigration.

ḥikmah: wisdom

ḥujjah: proof

hūwa: the pronoun "he," made up of the letters *hā'* and *wāw* in Arabic.

ʿibādu 'l-Lāh: servants of God

ʿifrīt: a type of Jinn, huge and powerful.

iḥsān: doing good, "It is to worship God as though you see Him; for if you are not seeing Him, He sees you."

Ikhlāṣ: *al-*: sincere devotion

ilāh (pl. *āliha)*: idols or god(s)

ilāhīyya: divinity

ilhām—Divine inspiration sent to *awlīyāullah*.

ʿilm: knowledge, science.

ʿilmu 'l-awrāq: knowledge of papers

ʿilmu 'l-adhwāq: knowledge of taste

ʿilmu 'l-ḥurūf: science of letters

ʿilmu 'l-kalām: scholastic theology.

ʿilmun ladunnī: "Divinely-inspired" knowledge

imān: faith, belief.

imām: leader of congregational prayer; an advanced scholar followed by a large community.

insān: humanity; pupil of the eye.

insānu 'l-kāmil, al-: the Perfect Man; the Prophet Muhammad ﷺ.

irādatullāh: the Will of God.

irshād: spiritual guidance

ism: name

isma-Llāh: name of God

isrā': night journey; used here in reference to the night journey of the Prophet Muḥammad ﷺ.

Isrā'fīl: Archangel Rafael, in charge of blowing the Final Trumpet.

jalāl: majesty

jamāl: beauty

jamaʿa: group, congregation.

Jannah: Paradise.

jihād: to struggle in God's Path.

Jibrīl: Gabriel, Archangel of revelation.

jinn: a species of living beings, created out of fire, invisible to most humans. Jinn can be Muslims or non-Muslims.

Jumuʿah: Friday congregational prayer, held in a large mosque.

Kaʿbah: the first House of God, located in Mecca, Saudi Arabia to which pilgrimage is made and which is faced in the five daily prayers.

kāfir: unbeliever.

Kalāmullāh al-Qadīm: lit. Allah's Ancient Words, viz. the Holy Qur'an.

kalimat at-tawḥīd: lā ilāha illa-Llāh: "There is no god but Allah (the God)."

khalīfah: deputy

Khāliq, al-: the Creator, one of the 99 Divine Names.

khalq: creation

khuluq: conduct, manners.

Kirāmun Kātibīn: Honored Scribe angels.

lā: no; not; not existent; the particle of negation.

lā ilāha illa-Llāh Muḥammadun rasūlullāh: there is no deity except Allah, Muhammad is the Messenger of Allah.

lām: Arabic letter ل

al-Lawḥ al Maḥfūẓ: the Preserved Tablets.

laylat al-isrā' wa 'l-miʿrāj: the Night Journey and Ascension of the Prophet Muḥammad ﷺ to Jerusalem and to the seven heavens.

Madīnātu 'l-Munawwarah: the Illuminated city; city of Prophet Muḥammad ﷺ. Referred to as Madina.

mahr: dowry given by the groom to the bride.

malakūt: divine kingdom.

Malik, al-: the Sovereign, a Divine Name.

Mālik: Archangel of Hell.

maqām: spiritual station; tomb of a prophet, messenger or saint.

maʿrifah: gnosis.

māshāAllāh: it is as Allah Wills.

Mawlānā: lit. "our master" or "our patron," referring to an esteemed person.

maẓhar: place of disclosure.

miḥrāb: prayer niche.

Mikā'īl: Archangel of rain.

mīzān: the Scale which weighs the actions of human beings on Judgment Day.

mīm: Arabic letter م

minbar: pulpit.

miʿrāj: the ascension of the Prophet Muḥammad ﷺ from Jerusalem to the seven heavens.

Muḥammadun rasūlu 'l-Lāh: Muḥammad is the Messenger of God.

mulk, al-: the World of dominion

Mu'min, al-: Guardian of Faith, one of the 99 Names of God.

mu'min: a believer.

munājāt: invocation to God in very intimate form.

Munkir: one of the angels of the grave.

murīd: disciple, student, follower.

murshid: spiritual guide, *pīr*.

mushāhadah: direct witnessing

*mushrik (*pl. *mushrikūn)*: idolater, polytheist.

*muwwaḥid (*pl. *muwaḥḥidūn)*: those affiriming God's Oneness.

nabī: a prophet of God

nafs: lower self, ego.

Nakīr: the othe rangel of the grave (with Munkir)

nūr: light

Nūḥ: the prophet Noah ﷺ.

Nūr, an-: The Source of Light, a Divine Name.

Qādir, al-: the Powerful, a Divine Name.

qalam, al-: the Pen.

qiblah: direction, specifically, the direction faced by Muslims during prayer and other worship towards the Sacred House in Mecca.

Quddūs, al-: the Holy One, a Divine Name.

qurb: nearness

quṭb (pl. *aqṭāb)*: axis or pole. Among the poles are:

Quṭb al-bilād: Pole of the Lands

Quṭb al-irshād: Pole of Guidance

Quṭbu 'l-aqṭāb: Pole of Poles

Quṭbu 'l-a'ẓam: Highest Pole

Quṭbu 't-tasarruf: Pole of Affairs

al-quṭbīyyatu 'l-kubrā: the highest station of poleship

Rabb, ar-: the Lord

Raḥīm, ar-: the Most Compassionate, a Divine Name.

Raḥmān, ar-: the All-Merciful, a Divine Name.

raḥmah: mercy.

raka'at: one full set of prescribed motions in prayer. Each prayer consists of a one or more *raka'ats*.

Ramaḍān: the ninth month of the Islamic lunar calendar, the month of fasting.

rasūl: a messenger of God

Rasūlullāh: the Prophet of God, Muhammad ﷺ.

Ra'ūf, ar-: the Most Kind, a Divine Name.

Razzāq, ar-: the Provider

rawḥānīyyah: spirituality, spiritual essence of something.

Riḍwān: Archangel of Paradise.

rizq: provision, sustenance.

rūḥ: spirit. Ar-Rūḥ is the name of a great angel.

rukū': bowing posture of the prayer.

ṣadaqa: voluntary charity.

ṣaḥīḥ: authentic; term certifying validity of a hadith of the Prophet ﷺ.

Ṣā'im: fasting person (pl. *ṣāimūn*)

salām: peace.

Salām, as-: the Peaceful, a Divine Name.

as-salāmu 'alaykum: peace be upon you (Islamic greeting)

ṣalāt: Islam's ritual prayer.

Ṣalāt an-Najāt: prayer of salvation, done in the wee hours of the night.

Ṣamad, aṣ-: Self-Sufficient, upon whom creatures depend.

Saḥābah (sing., sahabi): the Companions of the Prophet, the first Muslims.

sajda (pl. *sujūd*): prostration.

ṣalāt: prayer, one of the five obligatory pillars of Islam. Also to invoke blessing on the Prophet ﷺ.

ṣalawāt (sing. *salāt*): invoking blessings and peace upon the Prophet ﷺ.

ṣawm, ṣiyām: fasting.

sayyid: leader; also, a descendant of Prophet Muhammad ﷺ.

Sayyidinā/ sayyidunā: our master (fem. *sayyidatunā:* our mistress).

shahādah: lit. testimony; the testimony of Islamic faith: *Lā ilāha illa 'l-Lāh wa Muḥammadun rasūlu 'l-Lāh* or "There is no god but Allah, the One God, and Muḥammad is the Messenger of God."

Shāh Naqshband: Grandshaykh Muḥammad Bahāuddīn Shāh Naqshband, a great eighth century *walī*, the founder of the Naqshbandi *ṭarīqah*.

shaykh: lit. "old man," a religious guide, teacher; master of spiritual discipline.

shifā': cure.

shirk: polytheism, idolatry, ascribing partners to God

ṣiffāt: attributes; term referring to Divine Attributes.

Silsilat adh-dhahabīyyah: "golden chain" of spiritual authority in Islam

sohbet (Arabic *suḥbah):* association: the assembly or discourse of a shaykh.

subḥanallāh: glory be to God.

sulṭān/sulṭānah: ruler, monarch.

Sulṭān al-Awlīyā: lit., "the king of the *awlīyā*,"; the highest-ranking saint.

sunnah: the practice of the Prophet ﷺ; that is, what he did, said, recommended or approved of in his Companions.

sūrah: a chapter of the Qur'an; picture, image.

Sūratu 'l- Ikhlāṣ: the Chapter of Sincerity, 114.

ṭabīb: doctor.

tābiʿīn: the Successors, generation after the Prophet's Companions.

tafsīr: to explain, expound, explicate, or interpret; technical term for commentary or exegesis of the Holy Qur'ān.

tajallī (pl. tajallīyāt): theophanies, God's self-disclosures, Divine Self-manifestation.

takbīr: lit. "*Allāhu Akbar,*" God is Great.

talqīn: to put a phrase on the tongue by recitation.

tarawīḥ: the special nightly prayers of Ramadan.

ṭarīqat/ṭarīqah: literally, way, road or path. An Islamic order or path of discipline and devotion under a guide or shaykh; Islamic Sufism.

tasbīḥ: recitation glorifying or praising God.

tawāḍaʿ: humbleness.

ṭawāf: the rite of circumambulating the Kaʿbah while glorifying God during Hajj and ʿUmrah.

tawḥīd: unity; universal or primordial Islam, submission to God, as the sole Master of destiny and ultimate Reality.

Tawrāt: Torah

ʿubūdīyyah: state of worshipfulness. Servanthood

ʿulamā (sing. *ʿAlīm*): scholars.

ʿulūmu ʾl-awwalīna wa ʾl-ākhirīn: knowledge of the "Firsts" and the "Lasts" refers to the knowledge that God poured into the heart of Muḥammad ﷺ during his ascension to the Divine Presence.

ʿulūm al-Islāmī: Islamic religious sciences.

ummah: faith community, nation.

ʿUmar ibn al-Khaṭṭāb ؓ: an eminent Companion of the Prophet ﷺ and second caliph of Islam.

ʿumrah: the minor pilgrimage to Mecca, performed at any time of the year.

ʿUthmān ibn ʿAffān ؓ: an eminent Companion of the Prophet ﷺ and his son-in-law, who became third caliph of Islam. Renowned for compiling the Qur'an.

walad: a child

waladī: my child

walāyah: proximity or closeness; sainthood.

walī (pl. *awliyā'*): saint, or "he who assists,"; guardian; protector.

wasīlah: a means; a special station granted to the Prophet Muḥammad ﷺ as intermediary to God in the granting the petitioner's supplications.

wāw: Arabic letter و

wujūd, al-: existence; "to find," "the act of finding," as well as "being found".

Yʿaqūb: the prophet Jacob ؑ.

yamīn: the right hand, used to mean "oath."

yawm al-ʿahdi wa'l-mīthāq: day of oath and covenant, a heavenly event before this life, when the souls of mankind were present before God where He took from each soul the promise to accept His Sovereignty as Lord.

yawm al-qiyāmah: Day of Judgment.

Yūsūf: the prophet Joseph ؑ.

zīyāra: visitation to the grave of a prophet, prophet's companion or saint.

www.ingramcontent.com/pod-product-compliance
Lightning Source LLC
Chambersburg PA
CBHW030326080526
44584CB00012B/735
* 9 7 8 1 9 3 0 4 0 9 5 9 0 *